Diseases of Travelers and Immigrants

A SCOPE® PUBLICATION

Scott B. Halstead, MD
Associate Director

Kenneth S. Warren, MD
Director
Health Sciences Division
Rockefeller Foundation
New York, New York

The authors assembled the information illustrated on the maps from several sources, including the *Morbidity and Mortality Weekly Report,* the *Weekly Epidemiological Record, Tropical and Geographical Medicine* edited by Doctor Warren and AAF Mahmoud, MD, and *Control of Communicable Diseases in Man* edited by AS Benenson, MD.

The photographs originally appeared in Peterson PK, Dahl MV: *Dermatologic Manifestations of Infectious Diseases.* Kalamazoo, Michigan, The Upjohn Company, 1982. The photographs are reproduced with permission from the authors.

Library of Congress Catalog Card Number 86-050471

ISBN 0-89501-017-8
©1987, 1988 The Upjohn Company, Kalamazoo, MI 49001

Contents

6

Preface

Travel is big business. Of the estimated 300 million people who traveled internationally in 1984, more than 8 million were US residents who visited developing countries. Those people were at unusual risk for one or more of the diseases described in this monograph. Even the 30 million US residents who visited Europe, the Soviet Union, or Canada were exposed to unusual diseases.

The term *traveler* should include military personnel returning from overseas assignments, itinerant airplane crews, business people, scholars, government workers, Peace Corps workers, geologists, anthropologists, archaeologists, and others who live outside the United States for months or years.

Immigrants as defined here include the 182 million foreign visitors who entered the United States in 1982. Of the visitors, 69% came from countries ecologically different from mainland United States. The term *immigrant* also embraces the more than 1 million refugees who have come from Southeast Asia, Cuba, the Caribbean, Central America, Iran, and parts of Africa since 1973. The group includes the several million unregistered aliens who live or work in the United States as well.

This monograph primarily concerns communicable diseases and will guide you toward the recognition and diagnosis of diseases of travelers or immigrants. The jet airplane enables infected travelers and immigrants to move during the asymptomatic incubation period and arrive in the United States before becoming acutely ill. By carefully noting where the patient has lived or traveled and assessing the patient's activities abroad, you can substantially narrow the list of possible diagnoses. By identifying the major organ system involved and the patient's complaint, you can refine the list of possible diagnoses still further.

To help with that process, Part 1 of this monograph includes 22 tables that list various diseases that travelers and immigrants may bring into North America. The diseases are categorized in several ways: body system (Tables 1 to 8), diseases that must be included in the differential diagnosis of exotic diseases (Table 9), geographic area or country where travelers or immigrants are likely to have caught specific diseases (Tables 10 to 20), incubation period (Table 21), and degree of risk of catching a disease (Table 22). Part 2 provides more detailed information about specific important communicable and noncommunicable diseases of travelers and immigrants and attributes of exposure and illness.

PART 1

General Principles

Principles of Diagnosis

TRAVEL HISTORY

The first and most important step in the diagnosis of diseases of travelers or immigrants is to ask about travel or residence abroad. "Where have you been?" is the key question. The distinction between travel and residence abroad should be explicit because people with limited knowledge of English may deny traveling but readily admit residence abroad.

Because some tropical infections (eg, African trypanosomiasis and cerebral malaria due to *Plasmodium falciparum*) cause unconsciousness and are rapidly fatal unless treated promptly, clinical suspicion can be a matter of life and death.

Determine the specific country or area in which your patient traveled, the environments the patient visited, the dates of travel, and the patient's specific activities. Knowledge of the patient's profession or occupation may be helpful. Ask the patient the questions listed below.

- In what countries have you traveled or lived?
- When?
- Did you visit or live in only large urban areas and visit only famous tourist attractions? Or, did you visit, eat, or stay overnight in rural areas?
- Did you eat in rural areas or sleep in native dwellings or tents? Were you protected by screens or mosquito nets? Were you bitten by mosquitoes or other insects? During the day or at night?
- What was your occupation abroad?
- Were you backpacking?
- Did you take gamma globulin, antimalaria medication, antibiotics, or antidiarrhea medication? How much and how often?
- Were you immunized? Against what?
- Did you take precautions against mosquitoes? Against impure food and water?
- Did you wade or swim?

PHYSICAL EXAMINATION

Perform a routine comprehensive physical examination. Pay careful attention to liver and spleen size, lymphadenopathy, scrotal size, edema, skin abnormalities, and neurologic deficits, particularly analgesia if it is a symptom of the disease suspected.

Examine the skin thoroughly in good light. Look for sores, eschar, or rashes that might be clues to the cause of the illness. High fever, prostration, shock, hemorrhagic manifestations, severe diarrhea, dyspnea, or varying degrees of central nervous system disturbances, including confusion and coma, warn that the patient may have acquired a disease outside the United States.

LABORATORY STUDIES

Acute illnesses

The most important life-threatening infection to rule out is malaria. More than 1,000 imported cases of malaria were reported by US physicians to the Centers for Disease Control (CDC) in 1984. Patients with acute malaria may have any or all of the following: sustained high fever, diarrhea, cough, dyspnea, prostration, or varying degrees of mental clouding. For patients with these symptoms, a complete blood count (CBC), including careful examination of thin and thick blood smears, may quickly establish a diagnosis and save lives. For more information about malaria, see page 62 ff.

Other life-threatening diseases can cause eosinophilia. For example, a severe intestinal helminth infection may cause eosinophilia that may indicate that worms are invading tissues. Helminth infections, especially disseminated strongyloidiasis, toxocariasis, or Katayama fever (acute schistosomiasis), may be severe or life-threatening.

Fecal smears from patients with acute diarrhea should be stained with Wright's stain and examined for inflammatory cells. In the feces those cells suggest that the patient may have shigellosis or amebiasis, both of which are treatable but severe, potentially fatal infections. (See also pages 86 and 107.) Stools should be examined for ova, protozoans, and helminths; and stool samples should be cultured for bacteria.

Subacute and chronic illnesses

Most diseases acquired by travelers and immigrants are not so life-threatening that they preclude taking the time to do a thorough work-up. Personnel in city, county, or state health departments; the CDC; and diagnostic microbiology laboratories in most medical schools can provide advice about the collection, storage, and shipment of specimens to be tested for evidence of exotic bacterial, parasitic, or viral infections. (For addresses of some of those agencies, see Appendix, pages 129-132.) The essential principles are:

Diseases of Travelers

- Collect specimens to be examined for bacterial, chlamydial, or rickettsial organisms before beginning antibiotic therapy.
- As early as possible during the acute phase, collect and store a serum specimen in a food freezer or ultra-low-temperature cabinet.

More detailed information appears in Part 2.

COMMUNICABLE DISEASES

In 1983, 10.2 million US residents departed by airplane for various foreign destinations excluding Mexico and Canada. Almost half of those US residents flew to countries where the risk of catching an exotic disease is great: 3.1 million went to the Caribbean and Central America, 0.6 million to South America, and 1.4 million to Asia and Africa. This total is small when compared with the 70 million US citizens who crossed into Mexico in 1982 for either brief or prolonged visits. Therefore, a substantial fraction of the US population is exposed annually to microbial flora or standards of hygiene that differ from those in the United States.

Most lifelong US residents who travel to developing countries lack immune protection against certain nearly ubiquitous communicable diseases (Table 9, page 25). Risk of acquiring these diseases may increase while US residents travel or live abroad. This may reflect the effects of changes in normal activities or life-style. For example, although the incidences of acquired immune deficiency syndrome (AIDS) are higher in certain North American cities than the reported incidences in many parts of the world, exposure to AIDS is a matter of individual risk factors. A vacation trip to the Caribbean or other areas where AIDS has been diagnosed, although at an incidence somewhat lower than in some US cities, may provide time for and access to sexual contacts with infected people. Consequently the risk of exposure may be the same as or higher than that in the United States. The same kind of heterosexual or homosexual activities will influence the risk of other sexually transmitted diseases.

Although the incidence of viral respiratory disease is as high in the United States as elsewhere in the world, colds are among the most frequent diseases of travelers for two reasons:

- increased close human contact, the most important form of which is probably handshaking, and
- encounters with viral strains for which the traveler lacks immunity.

Whether the stress of travel, including long hours of inactivity, new foods, new and anxiety-provoking experiences, and jet lag, singly or additively contribute to altered susceptibility is not known, but they are plausible causes in the increased occurrence of various illnesses associated with travel.

Travelers may be exposed to diseases that occur at higher

incidences in developing than in developed countries and to ubiquitous communicable diseases (Table 9) and to exotic diseases, which occur outside the United States and Canada (Tables 10 to 20). Exposure can happen in any of three settings.

The urban setting exposes people to agents transferred from person to person via aerosol, hand-to-hand contact (organisms of fecal or pharyngeal origin), contaminated food or water, sexual contact, or purposeful or inadvertent parenteral inoculation. The urban setting also exposes people to free-living organisms, such as mycobacteria, that multiply in urban environments.

In urban settings, tourists and business people stay only at tourist hotels in major cities, take excursions to rural or forested areas to see natural wonders, or go on safaris. Those people travel with a group and live in hotels and eat in restaurants that cater to tourists. This mode of travel does not protect travelers from agents that cause diarrhea or food poisoning. In fact, such organized travel may enhance the travelers' chances of having such illnesses, but organized travel does substantially reduce the risk of exposure to malaria.

Rural recreational settings provide short-term exposure to sylvan environments while people are picnicking, hiking, hunting, camping, exploring, and so forth. Short visits to rural areas expose travelers to the risk of bites by disease-carrying insects or infected animals, contact with infected animals, and exposure to organisms in soil, water, and dust. Recreation might include a swim in a lake or stream with exposure to skin-penetrating, water-borne bacteria or parasites. In areas of Africa, Latin America, and the Philippines where schistosomiasis is endemic and throughout much of the tropical world where *Leptospira* is endemic, swimming in a lake or stream exposes travelers to either disease.

People who live in rural environments for a long time are also exposed to certain diseases that occur with decreasing frequency in illegal aliens or refugees, immigrants or visitors, and North American citizens with unusual overseas occupations or life-styles. Outside developed countries, *rural* often implies low socioeconomic class, crowded living units, primitive sanitary measures, unusual dietary practices, or subsistence livelihood. Such environments are contaminated by human and animal wastes. Rural and some crowded urban environments may shelter disease-carrying insects, eg, *Triatoma* bugs and fleas. However, even prolonged rural exposure of US residents to such environments is not likely to provide exposure similar to that of a native child living in the same environment. A person who wears foot coverings or who avoids eating rare or undercooked meat, fresh vegetables, and unpeeled fruits can live in a human settlement teeming with eggs and infective larvae with minimal risk. For a child to follow such proscriptions is impractical.

Susceptibility and age factors can change the risk of acquiring an infection. *P falciparum* malaria infections are particularly virulent in susceptible adults. Hitchhikers, backpackers, students on tour around the world, and some solo travelers are at special risk.

MAJOR SPECIFIC COMMUNICABLE DISEASES

The most dangerous communicable disease of travelers or immigrants is *P falciparum* malaria, and the most common may be diarrhea; one third of travelers to developing countries will have diarrhea during the trip or within days of their return.

Because of high risk of death during the acute stage, *P falciparum* malaria must always be considered in patients with fever plus headache, cough, abdominal pain, diarrhea, hypotension, pulmonary edema, severe anemia, renal failure, or altered consciousness regardless of the duration or recurrence of fever. Malaria is the most common acute febrile disease imported into the United States. Delay or failure in diagnosing the disease has caused needless deaths. Commonly in the United States, malaria has been mistaken for an acute viral disease or a bacterial disease. Most clinical illnesses due to *P falciparum* malaria occur 2 to 3 weeks after bites by infected mosquitoes. However, prophylactic drugs that failed or that were not administered for the suggested 6 weeks after the patient left the area where malaria is endemic may delay onset. Drug prophylaxis and host susceptibility alter the normal disease course and complicate recognition still further.

Diarrhea is the most common disease of the traveler. The most important determinant of risk of diarrhea is the destination of the traveler. In most developing countries in Latin America, Africa, the Middle East, and Asia, risk ranges from 20% to 50%. Countries with intermediate risk include southern European countries and a few Caribbean islands; and countries with the lowest risk include the United States, Canada, northern Europe, Australia, New Zealand,

Japan, Cuba, and US and European possessions in the Caribbean. Travelers' diarrhea rarely threatens life.

The current consensus regarding prevention of diarrhea is that no medication should be taken. Antimotility agents actually increase the incidence of diarrhea, and halogenated hydroxyquinoline derivatives are not helpful in prevention and have serious neurologic side effects. Several antibiotics or chemotherapeutic agents are quite effective in preventing diarrhea, but their use must be weighed against possible side effects: allergic disorders, skin reactions, hematopoietic suppression, Stevens-Johnson syndrome, and teeth staining in children. Travelers might carry an antimotility drug or an effective antibiotic or both or a nonantibiotic antidiarrheal agent to use soon after the onset of diarrhea.

Travelers can treat most occurrences of diarrhea adequately by drinking as much fluid, including fruit juices and soft drinks, as they like and by eating salted crackers. Severe dehydration may require oral salt solutions (ORS) recommended by the World Health Organization or intravenous fluids. ORS-bicarbonate and ORS-citrate reverse acidosis and dehydration equally well. ORS-citrate powder is more stable at tropical temperatures than ORS-bicarbonate, and ORS-citrate is now the standard formulation that the WHO recommends. ORS should be taken continuously and in small amounts until diarrhea stops and urine volume returns to normal. Diarrhea with nausea, vomiting, abdominal cramps, or blood and inflammatory cells in stool should be treated with antibiotics. Travelers should be told to see a physician if they notice blood in the stool.

NONCOMMUNICABLE DISEASES AND OTHER PROBLEMS OF TRAVELERS

Care of the traveler includes counsel and preparation for the trip in addition to the diagnosis and treatment of any resulting or coincidental problems. Travel can be stressful and subject people to long periods of enforced immobility, often in the sitting position.

Probably the most frequent problems of travelers occur as the result of stress. Jet lag, fatigue, anxiety, or constipation plagues many travelers. In the patient with an overt or unexpressed chronic disease, travel may precipitate an acute episode. Serious problems such as myocardial infarction, arrhythmia, stroke, peptic ulcer, colitis, phlebitis, dermatitis, and assorted rheumatic or musculoskeletal disorders may be travel associated. The wise physician will counsel patients with chronic disorders to be prepared for stress-induced flare-ups or complications.

Other less serious problems commonly occur in travelers. In the tropics, the use of an appropriate sunscreen lotion on exposed skin, including the lips, is desirable. Encounters with poisonous land or marine organisms may cause discomfort. Jellyfish, man-of-war, and sea urchin stings can be temporarily disabling and sometimes cause blistering, necrosis, and secondary bacterial infections. Coral cuts tend to become infected by streptococci, and many infections are accompanied by severe secondary lymphangitis. Hazards on land include snakes, scorpions, centipedes, bedbugs, leeches, ticks, bees, and spiders.

TREATMENT

This book reviews general principles of treatment of the diseases described. More detailed descriptions appear in the most recent editions of textbooks of medicine, pediatrics, and infectious diseases. Information about parasitic diseases or drugs being investigated can be obtained by telephoning the Centers for Disease Control, Atlanta, Georgia, 404-329-3270, or at night, 404-329-2888.

Diseases of Immigrants

WHO IMMIGRATES TO THE UNITED STATES?

From 1980 to 1984, annual immigration into the United States averaged 566,600 people, two thirds of whom were women and children. Recent immigrants therefore constitute more than 1% of the US population. Most immigrants came from Asia, the Middle East, South America, Mexico, the Caribbean, and Central America.

A large proportion of legal immigrants to the United States are educated professionals or business people who lived in large cities abroad and who had life-styles and disease exposure profiles similar to those of US residents. Only exceptionally are such people infected with exotic organisms. Usually the prolonged waiting period required for issue of visas and the medical examination required by US embassies and consulates assure that immigrants from rural areas are not acutely ill.

Most aliens who visit the United States are not immigrants but visitors. Many will become patients while in the United States. In 1982, for instance, visitors made 182 million separate entries into the United States. A large proportion of those visitors enter the United States from Mexico, a country with a high incidence and prevalence of communicable diseases. Tourists, students, and business travelers from countries with exotic diseases are not usually from the lowest socioeconomic strata, urban or rural; and the incidence of exotic disease is likely to be quite low but not zero.

Illegal aliens are quite different. They come predominantly from the Caribbean, Mexico, or Central America and from low socioeconomic groups, both urban and rural. In the United States, many live in crowded urban ghettos in conditions that may amplify the incidence of new infections or exacerbate poorly controlled infections. The immigrants tend to be poorly nourished. Physicians may have to recognize nonverbal clues to patients' immigration status because they may not volunteer the fact that they are unregistered aliens. The probability of chronic exotic disease in this group is quite high.

The overlap between diseases of immigrants and diseases of such travelers as archaeologists, anthropologists, backpackers, geologists, and Peace Corps workers who live for prolonged periods in rural settings and who adopt local cultural and behavioral norms is important.

In summary, the incidence of obvious exotic diseases is likely to be quite low in immigrants as a whole. However, in unregistered alien children, the incidence of multiple gastrointestinal parasites, for example, will probably be extremely high.

COMMUNICABLE DISEASES

Immigrants may have the communicable diseases listed in Tables 9 and 10 to 20 (pages 25 and 26-36). The immigrants' risks for the diseases listed in Table 9 equal or exceed those for US citizens. Diseases likely to occur only in immigrants are shown in boldface type in Tables 10 to 20. This increased risk occurs almost exclusively in poor immigrants who have lived in rural areas and is related to poor hygiene, crowded living conditions, or exposure to zoonotic agents.

NONCOMMUNICABLE DISEASES

Visitors and immigrants come from populations of unique genetic composition with important cultural and dietary differences from those of North Americans and from environments that may differ substantially from those common in industrialized countries. For those and a multitude of other reasons, some identified and some not, the profile of noncommunicable diseases varies widely in residents of different countries around the world.

In general, the visitor or immigrant from non-Western countries can be expected to express various genetic disorders and neoplastic diseases different from those in North America. For example, the visitors and immigrants have generally low incidences of coronary artery disease, rather high incidences of cerebrovascular disease, and substantially higher incidences of anemia and nutritional or deficiency diseases and of hepatitis B carriers than the US population.

Genetic disorders

Many genetic diseases occur at about the same frequency in developing countries as elsewhere. Inherited anemias occur commonly in some tropical countries, probably because heterozygous carriers have been protected against *P falciparum* malaria. They may have glucose-6-phosphate dehydrogenase deficiency, which is important because it causes acute hemolytic anemia in patients taking the drugs often used to treat tropical diseases; and it may also cause anemia during various intercurrent illnesses. The carriers also have hemoglobinopathies such as sickle cell anemia or trait, hemoglobin C and E disorders, and the thalassemias.

Sickle cell disease is an important cause of vaso-occlusive and hemolytic episodes in people born in West or Central Africa and portions of the Arabian peninsula and India. People with hemoglobin C live mainly in West Africa and also in North Africa and other Mediterranean countries. Patients who are homozygous suffer from mild anemia and splenomegaly. Hemoglobin E is the most common hemoglobin variant in the world. It occurs at high frequency throughout Southeast Asia, India, and parts of the Middle East. People who are homozygous have mild anemia without splenomegaly. The chief problem is caused by interactions of hemoglobin E with α-thalassemia. α-Thalassemia is common in West Africa and part of the Mediterranean and from southern China to the Indonesian archipelago.

Clinical β-thalassemia occurs as a homozygous disease in combination with inherited abnormal hemoglobin types. β-Thalassemia occurs from the Mediterranean and North Africa, West Africa, the Middle East, eastern Europe, part of the Soviet Union to the Indian subcontinent, to southern Asia and southern China. Homozygous disease usually appears in the first year of life with failure to thrive, poor feeding, intermittent fever, or failure to recover from infectious diseases.

Glucose-6-phosphate dehydrogenase (G-6-PD) deficiency is widespread in Africa, the Middle East, Southeast Asia, and around the Mediterranean. Several genetic variations of the deficiency have been identified. Some patients are sensitive to drugs that form free radicals or oxidize hemoglobin. The drugs include among others the aminoquinolines, sulfones, sulfonamides, nitrofurans, aspirin, phenacetin, quinine, chloramphenicol, probenecid, dimercaprol, and vitamin K.

Neoplastic diseases

Although neoplastic diseases are generally regarded as noncommunicable, at least some that occur at high rates outside industrialized communities may have an infectious origin, which may explain their unique geographic distributions. The cancers include primary hepatocellular carcinoma, which occurs at high incidences in West, Central, and East Africa; through the Middle East; the Indian subcontinent; and southern and northern Asia, a distribution that roughly coincides with high rates of hepatitis B viral surface antigenemia. Nasopharyngeal carcinoma, a disease of southern China and Taiwan, is frequently associated with antibodies for the Epstein-Barr (EB) virus. A similar although closer association links EB virus with Burkitt's lymphoma distributed through much of East Africa. Certain forms of acute lymphatic leukemias have been directly related to the human T cell leukemia virus, HTLV-I. The leukemias, antibodies, and the virus are distributed in southern Japan, Okinawa, parts of South America, and Africa.

Neoplastic diseases with unusual geographic distribution but without current evidence of infectious origin include Kaposi's sarcoma of Central and West Africa and the Mediterranean region; stomach cancer common in Japan, China, and parts of Scandinavia; esophageal cancer that occurs at high frequency in parts of China; and bladder cancer that occurs in Africa and may be associated with chronic *Schistosoma haematobium* infections.

NUTRITIONAL DEFICIENCY DISEASES

Iron, vitamin B_{12}, folic acid, and iodine are the nutritional deficiencies most likely to occur among visitors or immigrants to the United States. Iron deficiency can be caused by helminth infections. The fish tapeworm, *Diphyllobothrium latum*, and bacterial overgrowth of the small bowel may impair absorption of vitamin B_{12}. Vitamin B_{12} absorption may also be impaired in patients with tropical sprue. Folic acid deficiencies also occur in patients with various forms of malabsorption.

As many as 200 million people may have endemic goiters. Iodine deficiency caused by low iodine concentrations in drinking water or low consumption of marine products is the most common cause. Goiters occur most commonly in central or mountainous areas of Africa and Southeast Asia although iodine-blocking substances in water of the Cauca Valley of Colombia and the cyogenic glycoside in cassava eaten in Central Africa may contribute to iodine deficiency.

IMMUNE OR IDIOPATHIC DISORDERS

Lupus erythematosus occurs at a higher frequency in people of southern Chinese ancestry than in other populations. Rheumatic carditis and rheumatic heart disease are highly prevalent among rural residents of most developing countries.

Differential Diagnosis

Incubation periods (Table 21, page 37), general risk of catching the diseases (Table 22, page 38), the geographic area from which the traveler or immigrant returned (Tables 10-20, pages 26-36), the environment in which the traveler or immigrant lived abroad, and the early signs and symptoms of traveler's or immigrant's diseases (Tables 1 to 8, pages 20-24) provide clues to the diagnosis.

In Part 2 you will find brief sketches of important diseases ordered by organ system and alphabetically by disease name. We have emphasized the diseases with which US family practitioners, internists, or pediatricians would have had little or no experience and perhaps little or no instruction during their training. Common traveler's diseases such as diarrhea, food poisoning, and gastroenteritis are included for the convenience of the medical student and physician.

Selected reading

Advisory Memoranda. Statistical Abstract of the United States, ed 105. US Department of Health and Human Services, Centers for Disease Control, Atlanta.

Arendt J, Marks V: Physiological changes underlying jet lag. *Br Med J* 1982; 284:144-146.

Brown KR, Phillips SM: Tropical diseases of importance to the traveler. *Adv Intern Med* 1984;29:59-84.

Canizares O (ed): *Clinical Tropical Dermatology*. Oxford, England, Blackwell Scientific Publications, Inc, 1975.

Cossar JH, Reid D, Grist NR, et al: Illness associated with travel: A ten year review. *Travel Med Int* 1985;3:13-18.

Craig CF: *Clinical Parasitology*. Revised by Faust EC, Russell PF. Philadelphia, Lea & Febiger, 1964.

Failmezger TC: A clinical survey of skin diseases in selected Latin American countries. *Int J Dermatol* 1978;17:583-591.

George CF: Poisoning by animals. II. Arthropods and marine animals. *Travel Med Int* 1983;1:105-107.

Gove S, Slutkin G: Infectious diseases of travelers and immigrants. *Emerg Med Clin* 1984;2:587-622.

Grufferman S, Raab-Taub N, Marvin K, et al: Burkitt's lymphoma and other non-Hodgkin's lymphomas in adults exposed to a visitor from Africa. *N Engl J Med* 1985;313:1525-1529.

Health Information for International Travel 1985, US Department of Health and Human Services publication No. (CDC) 85-8280. Atlanta, Centers for Disease Control, 1985.

Hunter GW III, Swartzwelder JC, Clyde DF: *Tropical Medicine*, ed 5. Philadelphia, WB Saunders Co, 1976.

Kusumi RK: Medical aspects of air travel. *Am Fam Physician* 1981; 23:125-129.

Mandell GL, Douglas RG Jr, Bennett JE (eds): *Principles and Practice of Infectious Diseases*, ed 2. New York, John Wiley & Sons, 1985.

Morbidity and Mortality Weekly Report. Centers for Disease Control, Atlanta.

Perry IC: Air travel fatigue. *Travel Med Int* 1983;1:18-21.

Regional Breakdown of World Tourism Statistics, 1977-1981. Madrid, World Tourism Organization, 1982.

Steffen R: Epidemiology of health impairments during intercontinental travel. *Travel Med Int* 1985;3:76-79.

Steffen R, van der Linde F: Intercontinental travel and its effect on pre-existing illnesses. *Aviat Space Environ Med* 1981;52:57-58.

Thomson RB Jr, Haas RA, Thompson JH Jr: Intestinal parasites: The necessity of examining multiple stool specimens. *Mayo Clin Proc* 1984; 59:641-642.

Table 1

Early systemic signs or symptoms caused by diseases of travelers, visitors, or immigrants.

Systemic

Signs or symptoms	Possible causes
Anemia	Histoplasmosis **Hookworm** Tropical sprue **Visceral leishmaniasis**
Acute fever	Dengue Ebola-Marburg hemorrhagic fever
Chronic fever	Actinomycosis AIDS Brucellosis Histoplasmosis **Relapsing fever** Typhoid fever
Recurring fever	Malaria
Exanthem with fever	Chikungunya Childhood exanthem Dengue Enterovirus exanthems Rickettsioses (eg, boutonneuse fever)
Fever accompanying hemorrhage or shock	Congo-Crimean hemorrhagic fever Dengue **Dengue hemorrhagic fever** **Dengue shock syndrome** Ebola-Marburg hemorrhagic fever Hemorrhagic fever with renal syndrome Lassa fever Leptospirosis
Life-threatening signs (eg, coma, septicemia)	**Anthrax** **Chagas' disease** Congo-Crimean hemorrhagic fever **Dengue hemorrhagic fever** **Dengue shock syndrome** Ebola-Marburg hemorrhagic fever Hemorrhagic fever with renal syndrome Impending sudden unexplained death of adults
Lymphedema	Filariasis

Immigrants are more likely than travelers to have the diseases shown in **boldface** type.

Table 2

Early cardiovascular signs or symptoms caused by diseases of travelers, visitors, or immigrants.

Cardiovascular System

Signs or symptoms	Possible causes
Heart murmur	Chagas' disease Enteroviral carditis
Myocarditis	Rheumatic heart disease Trichinosis

Table 3

Early central nervous system signs or symptoms caused by diseases of travelers, visitors, or immigrants.

Central Nervous System

Signs or symptoms	Possible causes
Altered mentation	Acute psychosis
Coma	Cerebral malaria (P falciparum) Impending sudden unexplained death of adults Japanese encephalitis Meningococcal meningitis Rabies Tick-borne encephalitis
Localizing signs of a neurologic lesion	Angiostrongyliasis Botulism Cryptococcosis Cysticercosis Diphtheria Echinococcosis Gnathostomiasis Lyme disease Meningococcal meningitis Naegleria infection Poliomyelitis Schistosomiasis Tetanus

Table 4

Early ophthalmologic signs or symptoms caused by diseases of travelers, visitors, or immigrants.

Eyes

Signs or symptoms	Possible causes
Eye pain, swelling, or reddening	Chagas' disease (Romaña's sign) Hemorrhagic conjunctivitis Loiasis Onchocerciasis Trachoma Trichinosis

Table 5
Early gastrointestinal signs or symptoms caused by diseases of travelers, visitors, or immigrants.

Gastrointestinal System

Signs or symptoms	Possible causes	Signs or symptoms	Possible causes
Abdominal pain	Amebiasis	Hepatomegaly	Amebic liver abscess
	Anisakiasis		Chagas' disease
	Giardiasis		Clonorchiasis
	Hymenolepiasis		*Echinococcus multilocularis*
	Salmonellosis		Histoplasmosis
	Strongyloidiasis		Schistosomiasis
	Taeniasis		Visceral leishmaniasis
Diarrhea, acute	*Bacillus cereus*	Jaundice	Hepatitis, A, B, delta, non-A, non-B (epidemic and transfusion-related)
	Campylobacter		Leptospirosis
	Clostridium perfringens		Malaria *(P falciparum)*
	Escherichia coli		
	Rotavirus	Splenomegaly	Chagas' disease
	Salmonellosis		Chronic malaria
	Trichuriasis (heavy infestation)		Schistosomiasis
	Vibrio parahaemolyticus		Typhoid fever
Diarrhea, bloody	Amebic dysentery		Visceral leishmaniasis
	Campylobacter	Vomiting	*B cereus*
	Shigellosis		*Rotavirus*
Diarrhea, chronic	AIDS		Staphylococcal enterotoxin
	Clonorchiasis	Worms	Ascariasis
	Cryptosporidiosis		Taeniasis (tapeworm)
	Giardiasis		

Table 6

Early genitourinary signs or symptoms caused by diseases of travelers, visitors, or immigrants.

Genitourinary System

Signs or symptoms	Possible causes
Cervicitis	Chlamydial infection
	Moniliasis
	Trichomoniasis
Genital lesion	Chancroid
	Granuloma inguinale
	Herpes
	Syphilis
Hematuria	Schistosomiasis *(Schistosoma haematobium)*
Urethritis	Chlamydial and gonococcal infections

Table 7

Early respiratory signs or symptoms caused by diseases of travelers, visitors, or immigrants.

Respiratory System

Signs or symptoms	Possible causes
Cough	Ascariasis
	Bacterial and chlamydial respiratory infections
	Paragonimiasis
	Pertussis
	Psittacosis
	Tuberculosis
	Upper respiratory infections
Lesions visible on chest x-ray	Blastomycosis
	Echinococcosis
	Histoplasmosis
	Melioidosis
	Psittacosis
	Tuberculosis
Pharyngitis	Diphtheria
	Streptococcal infections
	Viral infections
Pneumonia	AIDS
	Anthrax
	Ascariasis
	Blastomycosis
	Coccidioidomycosis
	Histoplasmosis
	Legionellosis
	Paragonimiasis
	Plague
	Psittacosis
	Q fever
	Scrub typhus
	Strongyloidiasis
	Tuberculosis

Table 8
Early dermatologic signs or symptoms caused by diseases of travelers, visitors, or immigrants.

Skin

Signs or symptoms	Possible causes	Signs or symptoms	Possible causes
Analgesia	Leprosy	Swelling or erythematous lesions	Chagas' disease (Romaña's sign)
			Gnathostomiasis
Anal pruritus	Enterobiasis		Loiasis
			Lyme disease
Pruritus	Onchocerciasis		Pinta
	Toxocariasis		
		Ulcer, eschar, or abscess	Anthrax
Rash	Boutonneuse fever		Chagas' disease
	Chikungunya		Coccidioidomycosis
	Childhood exanthems		Cutaneous leishmaniasis
	Dengue		Lymphogranuloma venereum
	Enteroviral exanthems		Trypanosomiasis, African
			Scrub typhus
			Yaws

Table 9
Communicable diseases that must be considered in the differential diagnosis of diseases of travelers and immigrants.

Organ system	Diseases more prevalent in developing than in developed countries	Diseases that cause complaints similar to those of exotic diseases but are as prevalent in developed as in developing countries
Systemic	Brucellosis Enteroviral syndromes Hookworm Leptospirosis Typhoid fever	AIDS Histoplasmosis
Cardiovascular	Rheumatic heart disease	
Central nervous/ neuromuscular	Aseptic meningitis Poliomyelitis	Meningococcal meningitis Primary amebic meningoencephalitis Tetanus
Gastrointestinal including liver, spleen	Diarrhea Food poisoning Gastroenteritis Giardiasis Hepatitis A Hepatitis B (close contact transmission) Hepatitis, delta Hepatitis, non-A, non-B (epidemic) Salmonellosis Shigellosis Strongyloidiasis Trichuriasis	Enterobiasis Hepatitis B (parenteral transmission) Hepatitis, non-A, non-B (posttransfusion)
Genitourinary	Chancroid Granuloma inguinale Lymphogranuloma venereum Syphilis	Chlamydial infections Genital herpes Gonorrhea Nonspecific urethritis
Respiratory	Diphtheria Pertussis Tuberculosis	Blastomycosis Legionellosis Mumps Upper respiratory disease Viral respiratory disease
Skin	Leprosy Measles Rubella	Coccidioidomycosis Lyme disease Scabies Varicella

Table 10
Exotic communicable diseases in the Caribbean Islands and Mexico.

	Type of exposure		
	Urban living and travel Rural recreation Prolonged rural living	Rural recreation Prolonged rural living	Prolonged rural living
Caribbean Islands	Dengue	**Hookworm** **Schistosomiasis**	Sprue **Yaws**
Mexico	**Anisakiasis** Dengue	**Cysticercosis** Leptospirosis Malaria	**Chagas' disease** **Echinococcosis** **Leishmaniasis, cutaneous** **Leishmaniasis, visceral** **Leprosy** **Pinta** **Rabies** **Relapsing fever** **Tapeworm** **Trachoma** **Tuberculosis** **Typhus**

Immigrants are more likely than travelers to have the diseases shown in **boldface** type.

Table 11
Exotic communicable diseases in Central America and tropical South America.

	Type of exposure		
	Urban living and travel Rural recreation Prolonged rural living	Rural recreation Prolonged rural living	Prolonged rural living
Central America and tropical South America	**Anisakiasis** Dengue	Malaria Sandfly fever	**Chagas' disease** **Cysticercosis** **Filariasis** **Hymenolepiasis** **Leishmaniasis, cutaneous** **Leishmaniasis, visceral** **Leprosy** **Onchocerciasis** **Paracoccidioidomycosis** **Paragonimiasis** **Pinta** **Rabies** **Relapsing fever** **Schistosomiasis** **Taeniasis** **Trachoma** **Tuberculosis** **Yaws** **Yellow fever**

Immigrants are more likely than travelers to have the diseases shown in **boldface** type.

Table 12
Exotic communicable diseases in temperate South America and the Andes Mountains.

	Type of exposure		
	Urban living and travel Rural recreation Prolonged rural living	Rural recreation Prolonged rural living	Prolonged rural living
Temperate South America			**Chagas' disease** **Echinococcosis** **Typhus**
Andes Mountains			**Bartonellosis** **Brucellosis** **Plague**

Immigrants are more likely than travelers to have the diseases shown in **boldface** type.

Table 13
Exotic communicable diseases in Europe and the western Union of Soviet Socialist Republics.*

	Type of exposure		
	Urban living and travel Rural recreation Prolonged rural living	Rural recreation Prolonged rural living	Prolonged rural living
Europe		Boutonneuse fever **Tick-borne encephalitis**	**Babesiosis** **Diphyllobothriasis** **Hydatid disease** **Legionellosis**
Union of Soviet Socialist Republics (western)	Giardiasis	Lyme disease **Tick-borne encephalitis**	**Babesiosis** **Congo-Crimean hemorrhagic fever** **Diphyllobothriasis** **Hemorrhagic fever with renal syndrome** **Leishmaniasis** **Plague**

Immigrants are more likely than travelers to have the diseases shown in **boldface** type.
*For information about the Soviet Far East, see Table 18.

Table 14
Exotic communicable diseases in Africa.

	Type of exposure		
	Urban living and travel Rural recreation Prolonged rural living	Rural recreation Prolonged rural living	Prolonged rural living
North Africa		Boutonneuse fever **Hookworm** Malaria	**Anthrax** **Brucellosis** **Congo-Crimean hemorrhagic fever** **Dracunculiasis** **Hydatid disease** **Hymenolepiasis** **Leishmaniasis** **Plague** **Relapsing fever** **Schistosomiasis** **Taeniasis** **Trachoma** **Tuberculosis**
East, West, and Central Africa	AIDS Dengue	Ebola-Marburg hemorrhagic fever **Hookworm** Lassa fever Malaria **Schistosomiasis** **Strongyloidiasis**	**Anthrax** **Boutonneuse fever** **Cholera** **Congo-Crimean hemorrhagic fever** **Dracunculiasis** **Leprosy** **Loiasis** **Onchocerciasis** **Paragonimiasis** **Plague** **Rabies** **Relapsing fever** **Rift Valley fever** **Schistosomiasis** **Trachoma** **Trypanosomiasis** **Tuberculosis** **Typhus** **Yaws**
South Africa			**Anthrax** Ebola-Marburg hemorrhagic fever **Rift Valley fever** **Schistosomiasis**

Immigrants are more likely than travelers to have the diseases shown in **boldface** type.

Table 15
Exotic communicable diseases in the Middle East.

	Type of exposure		
	Urban living and travel Rural recreation Prolonged rural living	Rural recreation Prolonged rural living	Prolonged rural living
Middle East		Boutonneuse fever **Hookworm** Malaria	**Anthrax** **Brucellosis** **Congo-Crimean hemorrhagic fever** **Dracunculiasis** **Hydatid disease** **Hymenolepiasis** **Leishmaniasis** **Plague** **Relapsing fever** **Schistosomiasis** **Taeniasis** **Trachoma** **Tuberculosis**

Immigrants are more likely than travelers to have the diseases shown in **boldface** type.

Table 16
Exotic communicable diseases in the Indian subcontinent and Sri Lanka.

	Type of exposure		
	Urban living and travel Rural recreation Prolonged rural living	Rural recreation Prolonged rural living	Prolonged rural living
Indian subcontinent and Sri Lanka	Dengue Hepatitis, non-A, non-B (epidemic)	**Hookworm** Malaria **Strongyloidiasis**	**Boutonneuse fever** **Cholera** **Filariasis** **Hymenolepiasis** **Japanese encephalitis** **Leishmaniasis, cutaneous** **Leishmaniasis, visceral** **Leprosy** **Rabies** **Scrub typhus** **Trachoma** **Tuberculosis**

Immigrants are more likely than travelers to have the diseases shown in **boldface** type.

Table 17
Exotic communicable diseases in Southeast Asia.

	Type of exposure		
	Urban living and travel Rural recreation Prolonged rural living	Rural recreation Prolonged rural living	Prolonged rural living
Southeast Asia	Dengue Hepatitis, non-A, non-B	**Hookworm** Malaria **Strongyloidiasis**	**Angiostrongyliasis** **Anthrax** **Capillariasis** **Cholera** **Clonorchiasis** **Dengue** **Fasciolopsiasis** **Filariasis** **Gnathostomiasis** **Leprosy** Melioidosis **Opisthorchiasis** **Paragonimiasis** **Rabies** **Schistosomiasis** **Scrub typhus** **Taeniasis** **Tuberculosis**

Immigrants are more likely than travelers to have the diseases shown in **boldface** type.

Table 18
Exotic communicable diseases in China, Korea, and the Soviet Far East.*

	Type of exposure		
	Urban living and travel Rural recreation Prolonged rural living	Rural recreation Prolonged rural living	Prolonged rural living
China and Korea	Dengue	**Hookworm** Malaria **Strongyloidiasis**	**Clonorchiasis** **Fasciolopsiasis** **Filariasis** **Hemorrhagic fever with renal syndrome** **Japanese encephalitis** **Leprosy** **Paragonimiasis** **Rabies** **Schistosomiasis** **Trachoma** **Tuberculosis**
Soviet Far East			**Hemorrhagic fever with renal syndrome** **Japanese encephalitis** **Tick-borne encephalitis**

Immigrants are more likely than travelers to have the diseases shown in **boldface** type.

*For information about the western USSR, see Table 13.

Table 19
Exotic communicable diseases in Japan.

	Type of exposure		
	Urban living and travel Rural recreation Prolonged rural living	Rural recreation Prolonged rural living	Prolonged rural living
Japan		**Anisakiasis**	**Hemorrhagic fever with renal syndrome** **Japanese encephalitis** **Schistosomiasis** **Scrub typhus**

Immigrants are more likely than travelers to have the diseases shown in **boldface** type.

Table 20
Exotic communicable diseases in Australia, New Zealand, and the Pacific Islands.

	Type of exposure		
	Urban living and travel Rural recreation Prolonged rural living	Rural recreation Prolonged rural living	Prolonged rural living
Australia and **New Zealand**	Dengue Ross River fever	Lyme disease	**Hymenolepiasis** Melioidosis **Murray Valley encephalitis** **Q fever**
Pacific Islands	**Ciguatera poisoning** Dengue Ross River fever **Scombroid poisoning**	Hookworm Strongyloidiasis	**Angiostrongyliasis** **Filariasis** **Leprosy** **Yaws**

Immigrants are more likely than travelers to have the diseases shown in **boldface** type.

Table 21
Usual incubation periods of diseases of travelers and immigrants.

Short (about 1 week or less)	Intermediate (1 to 4 weeks)	Long (1 to 6 months)	Very long (2 months to years)
Anthrax	Amebiasis	Ascariasis	AIDS
Boutonneuse fever	Brucellosis	Blastomycosis	Cysticercosis
Chancroid	Chagas' disease	Hepatitis B	Echinococcosis
Chikungunya	Giardiasis	Hepatitis, delta	Filariasis
Chlamydial infections	Hemorrhagic fever	Hepatitis, non-A, non-B	Fluke infections
Congo-Crimean	with renal syndrome	(posttransfusion)	Leishmaniasis, visceral
hemorrhagic fever	Hepatitis A	Leishmaniasis, cutaneous	Leprosy
Dengue	Hepatitis, non-A, non-B	Loiasis	Schistosomiasis
Diarrhea, acute	(epidemic)	Malaria	Trypanosomiasis,
Ebola-Marburg	Katayama fever	Melioidosis	African (Gambian)
hemorrhagic fever	Lassa fever	Pinta	
Food poisoning	Leptospirosis	Rabies	
Gonorrhea	Lyme disease	Taeniasis	
Herpes genitalis	Lymphogranuloma venereum	Trachoma (scarring)	
Histoplasmosis	Malaria	Trichuriasis	
Legionellosis	Pertussis	Tropical sprue	
Plague	Q fever	Yaws	
Psittacosis	Strongyloidiasis		
Relapsing fever	Syphilis		
Salmonellosis	Trypanosomiasis,		
Tetanus	African (Rhodesian)		
Trypanosomal chancre	Typhoid fever		
Viral gastroenteritis	Typhus, louse-borne		
Yellow fever	Typhus, murine		
	Typhus, scrub		

Table 22
Travelers' relative risk of catching certain communicable diseases in developing countries.

High: More than one case in ten travelers	Moderate: More than one case in 200 travelers but less than one case in ten travelers	Low: More than one case in 1,000 travelers but less than one case in 200 travelers	Very low: Less than one case in 1,000 travelers
Diarrhea	Dengue	Acute hemorrhagic conjunctivitis	Actinomycosis
Upper respiratory infection	Enteroviral infection	Amebiasis	AIDS
	Food poisoning	Ascariasis	Angiostrongyliasis
	Gastroenteritis	Childhood viral infections	Anisakiasis
	Giardiasis	Chickenpox	Anthrax
	Hepatitis A	Measles	Blastomycosis
	Malaria without prophylaxis	Mumps	Boutonneuse fever
	Salmonellosis	Poliomyelitis	Chagas' disease
	Sexually transmitted diseases	Enterobiasis	Chikungunya
	Chlamydial infection	Hepatitis B	Clonorchiasis
	Gonorrhea	Hepatitis, non-A, non-B (epidemic)	Coccidioidomycosis
	Herpes simplex	Leptospirosis	Congo-Crimean hemorrhagic fever
	Nonspecific urethritis	Scabies	Cryptosporidiosis
	Shigellosis	Sexually transmitted diseases	Diphtheria
		Chancroid	Ebola-Marburg hemorrhagic fever
		Syphilis	Echinococcosis
		Strongyloidiasis	Filariasis
		Trichuriasis	Gnathostomiasis
		Tropical sprue	Histoplasmosis
		Tuberculosis	Hookworm
		Typhoid fever	Legionellosis
			Lymphogranuloma venereum
			Malaria with prophylaxis
			Melioidosis
			Paragonimiasis
			Pertussis
			Pinta
			Plague
			Psittacosis
			Q fever
			Rabies
			Relapsing fever
			Schistosomiasis
			Toxocariasis
			Trachoma
			Trichinosis
			Trypanosomiasis
			Typhus
			Yaws
			Yellow fever

PART 2

Important Diseases
of Travelers and Immigrants

Systemic Diseases

ACQUIRED IMMUNE DEFICIENCY SYNDROME (AIDS)

Agent
A retrovirus, human immunodeficiency virus (HIV), formerly called human T cell lymphotropic virus type III lymphadenopathy-associated virus (HTLV-III/LAV)

Distribution
Worldwide

Epidemiology
AIDS was first described in the United States in 1981, but the disease occurred before that in Zaire and other Central African countries and Haiti. AIDS has spread rapidly in the homosexual community around the world and must be regarded as a global threat to travelers who are sexually active. Immigrants or visitors, especially from Central and East Africa, may have the disease.

In the United States, 72% of AIDS patients are homosexual or bisexual men; 17% are intravenous drug abusers; 4% are Haitians; and 1% have hemophilia and receive multiple blood transfusions. Because in Africa nearly equal numbers of men and women have AIDS and the number of reports of heterosexual transmission is growing, AIDS may become a conventional sexually transmitted disease.

Clinical characteristics and course
Onset usually is insidious. The disease may be first recognized when the patient becomes infected with an organism often associated with an exotic disease such as *Pneumocystis carinii* pneumonia, chronic enteric cryptosporidiosis, disseminated strongyloidiasis, toxoplasmosis, esophageal candidiasis, cryptococcosis, tuberculosis, atypical mycobacterial infections, cytomegalovirus infections, herpes simplex infections, progressive multifocal leukoencephalopathy, Kaposi's sarcoma, or primary lymphoma of the brain. Nearly all AIDS patients with those infections or tumors die.

Diagnosis
Most patients with AIDS have specific antibodies to HIV.

Principles of treatment
Appropriate chemotherapeutic agents are used to treat local and systemic infections. Experimental treatment includes agents that interfere with retrovirus replication or that restore or mimic helper T cell activity.

Prevention
Until a vaccine becomes available, prevention of transmission is the only means of preventing AIDS.

Selected reading

Broder S, Gallo RC: Human T-cell leukemia viruses (HTLV): A unique family of pathogenic retroviruses. *Annu Rev Immunol* 1985;3:321-336.

Francis DP, Petricciani JC: Prospects for and pathways toward a vaccine for AIDS. *N Engl J Med* 1985;313:1586-1590.

Lane HC, Fauci AS: Immunologic abnormalities in the acquired immune deficiency syndrome. *Annu Rev Immunol* 1985;3:447-500.

Peterman TA, Drotman DP, Curran JW: Epidemiology of the acquired immunodeficiency syndrome. *Epidemiol Rev* 1985;7:1-21.

Sherertz RJ: Acquired immune deficiency syndrome. A perspective for the medical practitioner. *Med Clin North Am* 1985;69:637-655.

BOUTONNEUSE FEVER
(Marseilles fever, African tick fever)

Agent
Rickettsia conorii

Distribution
See Figure 1.

Epidemiology
In Europe and the Middle East, boutonneuse fever is a disease of travelers who frequent campgrounds, picnic areas, and hiking trails. The rickettsiae are transmitted by *Rhipicephalus sanguineus*, a dog tick living in the basins of the Mediterranean, Black, and Caspian Seas. Infection is spreading rapidly because European tourists take their dogs to infested camping sites. Various ticks that live on rodents are transmitting the rickettsiae throughout much of Africa and India. Rickettsiae are transmitted from tick to tick by transovarial and transstadial infection.

Clinical characteristics and course
After an incubation period of 5 to 7 days, a primary ulcer

Systemic Diseases

Figure 1. The distribution of boutonneuse fever.

Systemic Diseases

with a black center and a red areola appears at the site of the bite. The appearance of the ulcer is followed by fever and then a general maculopapular erythematous rash of the palms and soles. The infection is mild and rarely fatal even when not treated.

Diagnosis

A complement fixation test, an enzyme-linked immunosorbent assay (ELISA), or the Weil-Felix agglutination reaction will demonstrate a rise in specific antibody titers in serum drawn 2 weeks after onset when compared with serum drawn as soon possible after symptoms appear (paired sera). The rickettsiae can be isolated from eggs or a tissue culture into which the blood of a febrile patient has been injected.

Principles of treatment

Appropriate antibiotics will usually cure the infection.

Prevention

People in tick-infested areas should search for ticks frequently and remove them with steady, gentle traction and without crushing. Removing ticks from dogs minimizes the tick population near humans. Tick repellents may be helpful.

Selected reading

Font-Creus B, Bella-Cueto F, Espejo-Arenas E, et al: Mediterranean spotted fever: A cooperative study of 227 cases. *Rev Infect Dis* 1985;7:635-642.

CHIKUNGUNYA

Agent

Chikungunya virus
(Togaviridae, *Alphavirus*)

Distribution

See Figure 2.

Epidemiology

In urban areas of tropical Africa, India, Sri Lanka, and Southeast Asia, chikungunya virus is transmitted by the *Aedes aegypti* mosquito. The virus appears to be endemic in Burma, most of Indonesia, and Vietnam. About every 20 years, chikungunya pandemics have spread from an enzootic focus in eastern or Southeast Africa to India and then throughout Southeast Asia.

Clinical characteristics and course

Chikungunya begins 3 to 5 days after a bite by an infected mosquito. The patient's temperature rises sharply to 40° to 40.6°C, and a macular blush appears. Headache, gastrointestinal disturbances, anorexia, and malaise accompany the fever, the mean duration of which is 3 days. Arthralgias that begin with the onset of fever and continue for a few weeks after temperature has returned to normal may temporarily disable the patient. Stiffness and discomfort are particularly troublesome when the patient gets up in the morning, but chronic arthritis does not follow. Chikungunya is self-limited and rarely fatal.

Diagnosis

Hemagglutination-inhibition or serum neutralization tests demonstrate significant antibody responses in paired sera. In tissue cultures and suckling mice, the virus can be isolated from blood drawn during the acute phase.

Principles of treatment

Antipyretics and cold sponge baths may help to alleviate the fever, which can cause convulsions that may be a problem in children. Other treatment consists of bed rest and other forms of supportive therapy. Analgesics may be needed to control joint pain.

Prevention

The *Aedes aegypti* mosquito bites in the daytime and breeds in and near human habitation, such as hotels and restaurants, especially in tropical countries. People visiting marketplaces, schools, hospitals, or private homes during the day risk exposure. In countries where the infection is endemic or where an epidemic has begun, mosquito repellent should be used on all exposed skin surfaces.

Selected reading

Halstead SB: Arboviruses and their diseases. Pacific and Southeast Asia, in Feigin RD, Cherry JD (eds): *Textbook of Pediatric Infectious Disease*. Philadelphia, WB Saunders Co, 1981.

Systemic Diseases

Figure 2. The distribution of chikungunya.

Systemic Diseases

CONGO-CRIMEAN HEMORRHAGIC FEVER (CCHF)
(Central Asian hemorrhagic fever)

Agent
Congo virus (Bunyaviridae)

Distribution
See Figure 3.

Epidemiology
The likelihood that a US traveler will catch CCHF is small; but because the disease is easily transferred to health care personnel, it must be considered in the differential diagnosis of hemorrhagic fevers or life-threatening illnesses. Hares, rodents, insectivores, and ticks serve as reservoirs for the virus; and the Congo virus can multiply in sheep and goats. *Hyalomma* and *Boophilus* ticks transfer the virus to humans. Agricultural workers are at the greatest risk of catching the infection.

Clinical characteristics and course
Three to 12 days after infection with the virus, the patient experiences sudden onset of fever, weakness, malaise, irritability, headache, and myalgias. The fever may last 5 to 12 days. Vomiting, abdominal pain, and diarrhea may occur. The patient's face becomes flushed; and a hemorrhagic enanthem appears on the soft palate, uvula, and pharynx. Scattered petechiae appear usually on the trunk. Patients with severe infections bleed heavily from the gums, nose, lungs, kidneys, uterus, or intestines. Lymphopenia and thrombocytopenia are pronounced. Fatality rates vary from 2% to 50%.

Diagnosis
The diagnosis of CCHF is established by isolating the virus from the blood in an appropriate cell culture or test animal. Complement fixation, plaque reduction neutralization, and febrile agglutinins tests; an ELISA; or gel diffusion will demonstrate significant antibody titer responses in paired sera.

Principles of treatment
CCHF patients should be housed and treated in a high-containment setting, such as a specially designed room with laminar air flow exhaust. All health care personnel must wear caps, masks, gowns, and gloves. The patient's excreta should be decontaminated chemically or autoclaved. Treatment should provide physiologic support and intensive care.

Prevention
Travelers should avoid tick bites and in infested areas should search their whole bodies frequently for attached ticks, which should be removed promptly with gentle, steady traction and without crushing.

To prevent the spread of the infection, blood from patients suspected of having the infection should be handled as if it were highly infectious, and surgery and autopsies should be performed extremely carefully. Nosocomial outbreaks have followed surgery for severe gastrointestinal bleeding in patients with CCHF.

Selected reading

Viral haemorrhagic fever surveillance. Congo-Crimean haemorrhagic fever. *Weekly Epidemiol Record* 1984;59:311.

Leads from the *MMWR*. Congo-Crimean hemorrhagic fever – Republic of South Africa. *JAMA* 1984;252:2533-2537.

Viral hemorrhagic fever: Initial management of suspected and confirmed cases. *Ann Intern Med* 1984;101:73-81.

DENGUE, DENGUE HEMORRHAGIC FEVER, AND DENGUE SHOCK SYNDROME
(Breakbone fever)

Agent
Dengue viruses types 1, 2, 3, 4
(Togaviridae, *Flavivirus*)

Distribution
See Figure 4.

Epidemiology
Aedes aegypti mosquitoes transmit the dengue viruses in urban areas in most tropical countries. The mosquitoes breed in relatively clean water stored in and near restaurants and human housing. The mosquitoes bite during the day, usually in the early morning or late afternoon. Where multiple dengue serotypes are simultaneously or sequentially endemic, dengue hemorrhagic fever or dengue shock

Systemic Diseases

Figure 3. The distribution of Congo-Crimean hemorrhagic fever.

Systemic Diseases

Figure 4. The distribution of dengue.

Systemic Diseases

Figure 5. The early scarlatiniform rash of classic dengue.

Figure 6. A shower of petechiae that developed after a tourniquet was applied to a patient who had dengue hemorrhagic fever.

Figure 7. Morbilliform exanthem that can occur in a patient with dengue.

syndrome, both of which are severe, may occur, usually in children up to the age of 15.

Clinical characteristics and course

After an incubation period of 3 to 8 days, usually 4 days, fever begins abruptly. Many dengue patients also have retro-orbital headache, nausea, vomiting, diarrhea, anorexia, and malaise and an early macular blush (Figure 5) covering the whole body. Taste aberrations may be pronounced. During the fever, which lasts 4 to 5 days, patients may experience hyperesthesia of the skin of the whole body and swelling of the hands and feet. The fever curve may be diphasic; and as the fever abates, a maculopapular rubelliform exanthem (Figure 6) covers the whole body. Signs of minor bleeding such as epistaxis, petechiae (Figure 7), gum bleeding, and menometrorrhagia are common, but gastrointestinal bleeding and hematuria are rare. After the illness, many patients become depressed and weak, and they may have bradycardia.

In some patients, acute vascular permeability may occur. Fluids and small molecules such as albumin leak into the serosal cavities and tissue spaces. This is called *dengue hemorrhagic fever*. When it is accompanied by increased permeability and hypotension or narrow pulse pressure (less than 20 mm Hg), it is called *dengue shock syndrome*. Fatality varies between 1% and 20% in patients with shock. If the shock is not corrected, acidosis and often disseminated intravascular coagulation may cause severe hemorrhage in almost any site. Cerebral edema and intracranial bleeding may produce signs of encephalopathy.

Which form of dengue the patient gets appears to be related to immune status at the time of infection. The first, or primary, dengue infection is mild if the patient is at least 1 year old. If the second dengue infection is caused by a virus, particularly type 2, that differs from the virus that caused the first infection, the second infection can produce dengue hemorrhagic fever or dengue shock syndrome.

Diagnosis

Antibody response can be compared in paired sera with hemagglutination-inhibition, complement fixation, or neutralization tests or an ELISA. An immunoglobulin M (IgM)-capture ELISA can distinguish primary from secondary dengue infection.

Principles of treatment

Dengue hemorrhagic fever and dengue shock syndrome are

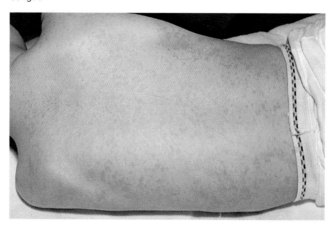

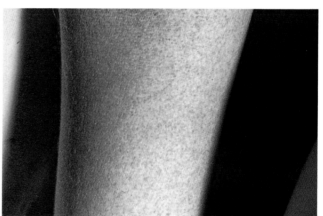

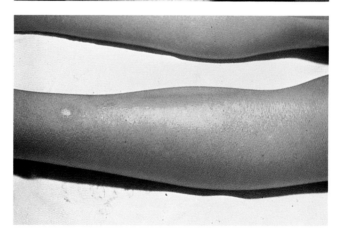

Systemic Diseases

acute medical emergencies. Replacement of fluid, electrolytes, plasma protein, red blood cells, and platelets and good intensive care minimize mortality. Before shock develops, oral rehydration salts may be useful (see page 90).

Prevention

The use of mosquito repellent on all exposed body surfaces is recommended in countries where the dengue virus is endemic and in other countries during epidemics. Visits to marketplaces, schools, hospitals, or private homes during daylight hours increase the traveler's risk of exposure.

Selected reading

Halstead SB: Dengue haemorrhagic fever – A public health problem and a field for research. Bull WHO 1980;58:1-21.

Halstead SB: The pathogenesis of dengue: Molecular epidemiology in infectious disease. The 1981 Alexander Langmuir Lecture. Am J Epidemiol 1981; 114:632-648.

Halstead SB: Selective primary health care: Strategies for control of disease in the developing world. XI. Dengue. Rev Infect Dis 1984;6:251-264.

Technical Guide for the Diagnosis, Management, and Control of Dengue Hemorrhagic Fever. Geneva, World Health Organization, 1986.

Viral hemorrhagic fever: Initial management of suspected and confirmed cases. Ann Intern Med 1984;101:73-81.

EBOLA-MARBURG HEMORRHAGIC FEVER
(African hemorrhagic fever)

Agents

Ebola virus and Marburg virus are closely related but antigenically dissimilar, filamentous viruses up to 14,000 nm long and unrelated to any other known infectious agents.

Distribution

See Figure 8.

Epidemiology

Indigenous residents of northern Zaire and western Sudan adjacent to northern Zaire have had infections with Ebola virus. In nearly all instances infection spread to hospital workers through person-to-person contact from infected blood, organs, or aerosol or from contaminated reusable needles and syringes. The virus is excreted in semen and may be spread by sexual intercourse, and infection has occurred as long as 7 weeks after the partner infected first had recovered.

Marburg disease was recognized in Germany in 1967 in a biologic products company among workers exposed to tissues of African green monkeys (Cercopithecus aethiops) from Uganda. In 1975 and 1982 infections occurred in backpackers traveling through Zimbabwe and in 1980 in two tourists in Kenya.

Clinical characteristics and course

After an incubation period of 3 to 12 days or less if the Ebola-Marburg virus is inoculated by a contaminated needle or syringe, fever begins suddenly and is accompanied by myalgia, headache, malaise, and pharyngitis. Those symptoms are followed by vomiting, diarrhea, maculopapular rash, hepatic and renal signs, and hemorrhagic diathesis. Leukopenia, thrombocytopenia, and abnormal transaminase concentrations occur commonly. The infection affects multiple organs, and those effects can only be detected with other clinical laboratory tests and x-ray studies. About 25% of patients with Marburg disease and 50% to nearly 90% of patients with Ebola disease die.

Diagnosis

Ebola-Marburg disease constitutes a public health emergency. Contact the Centers for Disease Control in Atlanta, Georgia, immediately for advice and assistance with diagnosis and management. Similar resources exist in Great Britain, Belgium, France, South Africa, and Australia. In other countries, contact the health ministry or the Division of Communicable Diseases of the World Health Organization in Geneva.

The inactivated antigens and the febrile agglutinins tests demonstrate specific IgM antibody in acute phase or paired sera. Electron microscopy can show the virus in blood or organs or in suitable tissue cultures or laboratory animals inoculated with blood or tissue from the patient. These procedures should be done only in containment laboratories with the most restrictive rating (P4).

Principles of treatment

Treatment is supportive, but antiviral chemotherapy is being evaluated. Apparently immune serum is ineffective once the illness has begun.

Systemic Diseases

Figure 8. The distribution of Ebola-Marburg hemorrhagic fever.

Systemic Diseases

Prevention

Strict isolation procedures must be instituted immediately. All hospital workers must wear caps, gowns, and gloves. Patients with Ebola-Marburg hemorrhagic fever can be housed in plastic isolators or rooms with laminar flow air exhaust and negative pressure if they are available. Patients' excreta, sputum, blood, and all objects, including laboratory equipment, with which the patient came in contact must be immersed in 0.5% sodium hypochlorite solution; or autoclaved and incinerated; or sterilized with gas. The patient's room and contents must be disinfected with sodium hypochlorite, a phenolic compound, or formaldehyde. All people who have had face-to-face contact with the patient must be identified, watched closely for 3 weeks, and have their temperatures measured twice daily. In the United States, a technician in a Vicker mobile laboratory will do all tests if arrangements are made with the Centers for Disease Control.

Selected reading

Viral haemorrhagic fever surveillance. Marburg and Ebola diseases. *Weekly Epidemiol Record* 1984;39:300-301.

FILARIASES

Agents

Wuchereria bancrofti (filariasis), *Brugia malayi* (filariasis), *Brugia timori* (filariasis), *Loa loa* (loiasis), *Onchocerca volvulus* (onchocerciasis)

Distribution

See Figures 9 and 10.

Epidemiology

Filariasis. Bancroftian filariasis is distributed throughout the tropics, and Malayan filariasis is distributed only in South and southeastern Asia. *B timori* is found in rural areas on Indonesia's eastern islands. As they bite humans, many species of urban and rural mosquitoes infected with *W bancrofti* or *B malayi* inject larvae into skin. The larvae mature to the adult stage in the lymph nodes in 6 to 12 months. Microfilariae pass from the fertilized females into the lymphatics and then into the bloodstream of the person bitten. The microfilariae mosquitoes ingest with a blood meal penetrate the mosquitoes' thoracic muscles, molt twice, and then pass to the proboscis. In most infected patients, the number of *W bancrofti* or *B malayi* microfilariae peaks from about 10 PM to about 2 AM except in the South Pacific, where the number of *W bancrofti* microfilariae peaks during the day.

Onchocerciasis. Onchocerciasis occurs in Africa, Central and South America, and Yemen. Female black flies (*Simulium*) transmit *O volvulus* infections to humans. When the flies bite, the larvae injected migrate into the connective tissue and mature in about 1 year into male and female worms that mate in nodules of fibrous tissue. The worms produce large numbers of microfilariae that migrate through the tissues. When ingested by the flies, the microfilariae become infective third-stage larvae within 10 days and move to the base of the labrum.

O volvulus infections tend to concentrate in one place. The epidemiology in Africa differs from that in Latin America. In Africa, flies breed in the fast-running streams and rivers and bite low on the body. In Latin America, flies breed in small streams and tend to bite the upper parts of the body.

Loiasis. Loiasis occurs in western and Central Africa. The *Loa* worm is transmitted to humans by the bite of tabanid flies of the genus *Chrysops*. The larvae migrate from the skin into connective tissue where they develop into threadlike worms in 12 months. The worms produce sheathed microfilariae that circulate in the blood during the day. Most infected patients are bitten during the day when they are at the edges of a rain forest. Dark skin and clothing, wood smoke, and movement attract the flies.

Clinical characteristics and course

Filariases are roundworm (nematode) infections of the lymphatic vessels and tissues.

Filariasis. Most infected patients are asymptomatic and may or may not have microfilaremia. The others may have filarial fever, lymphatic obstruction, or tropical eosinophilia. Most patients with filarial fever do not have microfilaremia. They do have acute lymphangitis or lymphadenitis or both. The lymphangitis originates from the draining nodes where the adult parasites are trapped. Patients also have acute high fever and transient local edema, backache, headache, and nausea. Acute episodes usually last a few days to a few weeks and recur several times annually. Lymphangitis or

Systemic Diseases

Figure 9. The distribution of filariasis caused by *W bancrofti*.

Systemic Diseases

lymphadenitis in patients with bancroftian filariasis usually occurs in the legs. Those patients may also have epididymitis and orchitis that may be associated with hydrocele. Only very small percentages of patients infected with *W bancrofti* or *B malayi* have hydroceles and even fewer have lymphedema. The arms of patients with Malayan filariasis are more likely than the arms of patients with bancroftian filariasis to be affected, and the genitalia of patients with Malayan filariasis are less likely to be affected than the genitalia of patients with bancroftian infections.

Chronic lymphatic obstruction with recurrent inflammatory episodes occurs in long-term residents of areas where the worms are endemic. Lymphedema may develop, and lymphatic varices may appear in the femoral, inguinal, and testicular regions. Chronic edema of the skin precedes thickening of the subcutaneous tissues, hypertrophy of the epithelium, and the appearance of wart-like lesions, irregular folding of the skin, and secondary infections characteristic of elephantiasis. Chylous ascites and pleural or joint effusions may occur when deep lymphatics are obstructed.

Tropical eosinophilia causes acute and chronic lung disease, which begins with paroxysmal coughing and wheezing generally at night and severe eosinophilia. The pulmonary changes are restrictive in almost all patients and obstructive in the others.

Onchocerciasis. O volvulus infections produce fibrous, firm nodules that are not tender, range from several millimeters to a centimeter or more in size, and are covered with freely moving skin. In patients with the African form of the disease, most nodules form over the bony prominences of the pelvis and on the chest wall, spine, and knees. In patients with the Latin American form of the disease, most nodules form on the upper part of the body, especially the head.

Severe pruritus may occur, particularly in people not native to the area where the worms are indigenous. A papular rash appears on the buttocks, and cutaneous lymphedema associated with leathery thickening of the skin may develop in patients with severe disease. The Latin American form may cause erythematous lesions on the face or upper trunk.

The most severe complications of onchocerciasis are impaired visual acuity and blindness, which usually develop over several years. Microfilariae can be seen in the anterior chamber or cornea, or patients may have punctate keratitis of the cornea. Atrophy of the iris is common.

Loiasis. The most striking sign of loiasis is transient, local subcutaneous edema known as a Calabar swelling. Although the swellings may occur anywhere, they are most common around medium-sized joints and areas exposed to trauma, such as the legs, hands, or orbits of the eyes.

The first signs of the disease are local pain or itching for 1 or 2 hours followed by swellings 10 to 20 cm in diameter. The swellings, which are not inflamed, last for several days and then slowly subside. Some adult worms produce prickling sensations when they migrate under the skin. The worms may be seen directly when they pass under the conjunctiva. Eosinophilia is common and may be quite severe.

Diagnosis

Bancroftian filariasis and Malayan filariasis, onchocerciasis, and loiasis are unlikely to occur except in long-term residents of certain areas where the infections are endemic. A definitive diagnosis is made by finding microfilariae or adult worms in the blood or tissues. Blood samples taken at midnight from patients with filariasis show all forms of the parasites whether or not life cycles produce peak numbers of worms during the night. A concentration technique should be used. Dilute 1 mL of blood in 10 mL of 4% formalin in water, shake the tube to hemolyze the red blood cells, and centrifuge the blood at 1,000 rpm for 5 minutes or filter the blood through a 5 micron membrane filter. Spread the deposit on a glass slide, dry it, fix in methanol for 3 minutes, dry again, and stain for 30 minutes with 10% Giemsa stain in phosphate buffer. When the patient does not have microfilaremia, the diagnosis must be made clinically; and the possible causes of the signs and symptoms are numerous.

To diagnose onchocerciasis, on the thighs, buttocks, and over the iliac crest and scapulae, with the tip of a needle raise small cones of skin about 3 mm in diameter, and cut off skin snips with a razor blade. Place the snips in drops of 0.9% NaCl solution, tease the tissue, allow it to stand for 2 to 4 hours, and look for microfilariae under a microscope. With a microscope, worms can also be identified in an excised nodule. Microfilariae can also be found in the urine of as many as 30% of patients and in the eye with the help of a slit lamp.

The microfilariae of *L loa* can also be found in blood, but the blood should be drawn between 10 AM and 2 PM. Some-

Systemic Diseases

Figure 10. The distribution of filariases caused by *B malayi*, *B timori*, and *L loa*.

●●●● *B malayi*
●●●● *B timori*
●●●● *L loa*

Systemic Diseases

times blood samples will contain adult worms. The worms can sometimes be seen in the eye.

When microfilariae cannot be detected in patients suspected of having filariases, diethylcarbamazine will produce characteristic pruritus in patients with onchocerciasis and systemic symptoms in patients with filariasis.

Principles of treatment

Several drugs kill microfilariae, but the effect is transient because adult worms continue to produce microfilariae. Therefore, treatment must be repeated at weekly intervals. At least one drug sometimes kills large numbers of worms, and that may cause acute inflammatory reactions to microfilarial antigens. The reactions can be treated with anti-inflammatory agents. At least one agent inhibits the expulsion of microfilariae from the gravid uterus of the adult worm but does not cause inflammatory response. The nodules of onchocerciasis can be removed surgically. Patients with ophthalmologic infections should consult an ophthalmologist experienced in treating filariases.

Prevention

The use of netting, screens, and mosquito repellent is important.

Selected reading

Bell D: Onchocerciasis now. *Br Med J* 1985;290:1450-1451.

Connor DH, Palmieri JR, Gibson DW: Pathogenesis of lymphatic filariasis in man. *Z Parasitenkd* 1986;72:13-28.

Higashi GI: Immunodiagnostic tests for protozoan and helminthic infections. *Diagn Immunol* 1984;2:12-18.

Negesse Y, Lanoie LO, Neafie RC, et al: Loiasis: "Calabar" swellings and involvement of deep organs. *Am J Trop Med Hyg* 1985;34:537-546.

Nelson GS: Onchocerciasis. *Adv Parasitol* 1970;8:173-224.

Sasa M: *Human Filariasis. A Global Study.* Baltimore, University Park Press, 1976.

HEMORRHAGIC FEVER WITH RENAL SYNDROME
(Hemorrhagic nephrosonephritis, epidemic hemorrhagic fever)

Agent
Hantaan virus
(Bunyaviridae, *Hantavirus*)

Distribution
See Figure 11.

Epidemiology
Field rodents (*Apodemus* species) in Korea and China excrete the virus in their urine, and the virus is probably transmitted to humans by aerosol in the spring and fall when the rodents invade places where humans live. Chinese and Korean immigrants and travelers who have worked or lived in rural areas may have contracted the infection. The virus also occasionally infects American military personnel in Korea, and infected laboratory animals have spread the virus to laboratory workers. A serologically related virus causes a milder disease, nephropathia epidemica, in Scandinavia, western Russia, and eastern Europe.

Clinical characteristics and course
After an incubation period of 12 to 16 days, hemorrhagic fever with renal syndrome begins with the abrupt onset of fever, conjunctival injection, backache, abdominal pain, nausea, vomiting, and prostration. Hemorrhages may occur on about the third day; and proteinuria, hypotension, and renal failure may follow. Most deaths result from uremia or urinary protein and fluid loss.

Diagnosis
Specific antibody titers increase, as is demonstrated in paired sera tested with neutralization fluorescent antibody tests or an ELISA. The virus can be isolated from blood or urine.

Principles of treatment
Carefully measure electrolytes and balance them. Restrict fluids during renal shutdown, and replace fluids during the diuretic stage. Renal dialysis may be necessary. An antiviral agent may reduce mortality.

Prevention
Control *Apodemus* near human habitation.

Selected reading

Hemorrhagic fever with renal syndrome – France. *MMWR* 1984;33:228, 233-234.

Systemic Diseases

Figure 11. The distribution of hemorrhagic fever with renal syndrome.

Systemic Diseases

Viral haemorrhagic fever surveillance. Expert Committee Meeting. *Weekly Epidemiol Record* 1984;59:197-199.

Public Health Laboratory Service. Haemorrhagic fever with renal syndrome: Hantaan virus infection. *Br Med J* 1985;290:1410-1411.

LASSA FEVER

Agent
Lassa virus *(Arenavirus)*

Distribution
See Figure 12.

Epidemiology
Lassa virus produces chronic infections in African rodents, principally *Mastomys natalensis*, which excrete the virus in the urine and feces. The virus is transmitted to humans most frequently by dust contaminated with rodent excreta. Humans excrete the virus in the urine or pharyngeal secretions, both of which are extremely infectious as is blood and autopsy tissue from infected patients. All material from infected humans endangers hospital and laboratory personnel and visitors. Patients with severe infections can be the source of nosocomial infections. Reusable needles and syringes also transmit the virus.

The virus is widely distributed in West and Central Africa. In some parts of West Africa, mild or asymptomatic infections are common.

Clinical characteristics and course
After an incubation period of 6 to 21 days, patients with Lassa fever experience the gradual onset of malaise, fever, headache, and abdominal pain followed by myalgia, nausea, vomiting, diarrhea, sore throat, and cough in succession. Other signs include pharyngeal reddening, enanthem on the pharynx and uvula, conjunctival injection, swelling of the face and neck, and hypotension. Patients with severe infections commonly have hemorrhagic manifestations, prostration, shock, pleural effusion, and neurologic signs. Usually patients have leukopenia, albuminuria, and hemoconcentration. Alopecia and deafness may develop during convalescence. In various studies, fatality rates vary from less than 5% to 90%. Prognosis is poor in patients with viremia of $10^{3.5}$ and aspartate aminotransferase concentrations of 150 units or higher.

Diagnosis
Attempts to recover virus from blood, urine, or infected organs should be made only in P4 biohazard laboratories. Diagnosis of Lassa fever can be made by demonstrating seroconversion in paired sera with the fluorescent antibody test or an IgM-capture ELISA.

Principles of treatment
Human plasma containing specific neutralizing antibodies is given with an antiviral drug; or the antiviral agent alone may be lifesaving if given during the first 6 days after the onset of fever.

Prevention
Prevent *Mastomys* rats from colonizing human dwellings.

Selected reading

Howard CR: Viral haemorrhagic fevers: Properties and prospects for treatment and prevention. *Antiviral Res* 1984;4:169-185.

Ishak KG, Walker DH, Coetzer JA, et al: Viral hemorrhagic fevers with hepatic involvement: Pathologic aspects with clinical correlations. *Prog Liver Dis* 1982;7:495-515.

Jahrling PB, Niklasson BS, McCormick JB: Early diagnosis of human Lassa fever by ELISA detection of antigen and antibody. *Lancet* 1985;1:250-252.

Lassa fever surveillance. *Weekly Epidemiol Record* 1984;59:198.

Tilzey AJ, Webster M, Banatvala JE: Patients with suspected Lassa fever in London during 1984. Problems in their management at Saint Thomas's Hospital. *Br Med J* 1985;291:1554-1555.

Viral haemorrhagic fever surveillance. Management of suspected cases. *Weekly Epidemiol Record* 1984;3:18-19.

LEISHMANIASIS, VISCERAL
(Kala-azar)

Agent
Leishmania donovani, Leishmania chagasi, Leishmania infantum

Distribution
See Figure 13.

Systemic Diseases

Figure 12. The distribution of Lassa fever.

Systemic Diseases

Figure 13. The distribution of visceral leishmaniasis.

Systemic Diseases

Epidemiology

Sandflies transmit *Leishmania*, intracellular protozoal parasites, from animals to man and back to animals. In man the parasite is an oval or rounded amastigote that changes to spindle-shaped promastigotes with flagella in the midgut of *Phlebotomus* sandflies that have taken a blood meal from an infected person. Within several days, the number of promastigotes increases, and they extend to the foregut from which they are transmitted to mammalian hosts by the sandfly's bite. The organisms live in Central and South America, the Mediterranean basin, the Middle East, the Sudan, Kenya, China, and parts of India. They live in rodents, domestic and wild dogs, and other mammals as well as in humans. The organisms can also be transferred by blood transfusions.

Clinical characteristics and course

Visceral leishmaniasis or kala-azar is caused by L donovani, which invades the reticuloendothelial cells of the spleen, liver, bone marrow, lymph nodes, and skin. Within a few days at the site of the bite, a cutaneous node develops (most often in patients with the African and Central Asian forms of the infection) and lasts for months. Systemic signs and symptoms begin insidiously after an incubation period of 2 to 6 months. The symptoms are dizziness, weakness, and weight loss. Most patients' fever increases twice daily. The spleen may be very large and firm but not tender, and patients may have general lymphadenopathy. Patients with chronic or untreated infection also have anemia, a tendency to bleed, jaundice, and hypoalbuminemia. Serum protein concentration increases substantially up to 10 g/100 mL, and the protein is virtually only immunoglobulin G (IgG). In untreated patients, mortality ranges from 75% to 90%. Patients usually die of intercurrent infection.

Diagnosis

Suspect visceral leishmaniasis in patients with prolonged fever, splenomegaly, anemia, leukopenia, or hypergammaglobulinemia. The best test is the examination of cells aspirated from bone marrow. Make several smears, air dry them, and stain with Giemsa stain. In the macrophages, look for Leishman-Donovan bodies, which are amastigotes. Cells are sometimes aspirated from the spleen or liver, but that could cause serious hemorrhage because the disease may impair clotting mechanisms. Other diagnostic tests are culture in special media of material aspirated from a patient or identification of the organism in the blood or spleen of hamsters inoculated with aspirated material.

Principles of treatment

In the United States, pentavalent antimonial compounds are available from the Centers for Disease Control. In patients with infections resistant to antimony, an aromatic diamidine or an antifungal antibiotic may be useful. In Kenya, leishmaniasis is drug resistant. No tests can confirm that the infection has been cured, and relapses occur.

Prevention

Travelers may be protected by using insect repellent and sleeping under fine mesh netting. No effective chemoprophylaxis or immunoprophylaxis exists.

Selected reading

Levitan H, Kantor I, Levitan LJ, et al: Leishmaniasis. *Mt Sinai J Med* 1984;51:274-282.

Pearson RD, de Sousa AR: Leishmaniasis in travelers. *Travel Med Int* 1985;3:208.

Pearson RD, deQuieroz-Sousa A: Leishmania species (kala-azar, cutaneous and mucocutaneous leishmaniasis), in Mandell GL, Douglas RG Jr, Bennett JE (eds): *Principles and Practice of Infectious Diseases,* ed 2. New York, John Wiley & Sons, 1985, pp 1522-1531.

LEPROSY
(Hansen's disease)

Agent
Mycobacterium leprae

Distribution
See Figure 14.

Epidemiology

M leprae bacilli that cause infections may spread from the nasopharyngeal mucosa of a patient, and crowded living conditions facilitate transmission. Worldwide, an estimated 12 million people have leprosy; but the bacillus is incubating in even more people with self-limited, undiagnosed infections. Leprosy is prevalent in India, China, Korea, tropical Asia and Africa, areas of Latin America, and some

Systemic Diseases

Figure 14. The distribution of leprosy.

Systemic Diseases

Figure 15. Lesions of borderline leprosy.

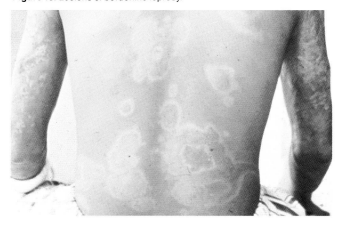

Pacific islands. A bacterium apparently identical to *M leprae* naturally infects armadillos in Mexico and the southwestern United States.

Clinical characteristics and course

Leprosy bacillus affects skin, peripheral nerves, and nasopharyngeal mucous membranes. A single hypopigmented macule may be the only sign of early leprosy, but the first symptom the patients notice may be anesthetic or paresthetic patches. The signs and symptoms of the disease can vary in a continuous spectrum from tuberculoid to borderline to lepromatous.

The incubation period for tuberculoid leprosy is at least 4 years and for lepromatous leprosy, 8 years. In the early stages, patients with tuberculoid leprosy have demarcated, sparse, hypoesthetic, and asymmetrical skin lesions. One or two peripheral nerves may be damaged and swollen.

Patients in the early stages of lepromatous leprosy have numerous, bilaterally symmetrical, erythematous nodules, papules, or macules. Patients may complain of having a stuffiness caused by crusting of the nasal mucosa. They may also have epistaxis. Conjunctivitis, iritis, and uveitis are common.

The intermediate form, borderline leprosy, causes clinical (Figure 15) and histologic changes from both polar types. It tends to shift toward the lepromatous form in untreated patients and toward the tuberculoid form in treated patients. Patients with advanced leprosy may have trophic ulcers, muscle wasting, paralysis, tenderness, and enlargement of the peripheral nerves.

Diagnosis

The demonstration of acid-fast bacilli in skin smears or skin samples taken for biopsy or of nerve involvement with acid-fast bacilli is diagnostic. Tissue should be taken from central and peripheral areas of the lesion and should include a block of fatty, subcutaneous tissue. Patients with lepromatous leprosy may fail to respond to intradermal inoculation of lepromin, heat-inactivated leprosy bacilli. Patients with tuberculoid leprosy and some normal people have granulomatous responses. Various antibody tests using capsular antigens are being evaluated for specificity and correlation with stage and type of infection.

Treatment

Drug treatment of leprosy can be complicated and lengthy. The World Health Organization recommends combinations of antibiotics. Patients with either form of the disease must be monitored for drug side effects and acute adverse reactions that require intensive supportive treatment. All leprosy patients require an array of supportive and rehabilitative measures. The United States Public Health Service Hospital for Leprosy at Carville, Louisiana, provides help with the treatment of leprosy patients.

Prevention

Because early diagnosis and treatment can prevent the spread of leprosy, people with subclinical infections should be identified and treated. People who have had close contact with a leprosy patient should receive prophylaxis. A leprosy vaccine is in an early stage of evaluation in human volunteers.

Selected reading

Bloom BR, Mehra V: Immunological unresponsiveness in leprosy. *Immunol Rev* 1984;80:5-28.

Buchanan TM, Young DB, Miller RA, et al: Serodiagnosis of infection with *Mycobacterium leprae. Int J Leprosy* 1983;1:524-530.

Levis WR: Treatment of leprosy in the United States. *Bull NY Acad Med* 1984; 60:696-711.

Stewart-Tull DE: Leprosy – in pursuit of a vaccine. *Vaccine* 1984;2:238-248.

Trautman JR: Epidemiological aspects of Hansen's disease. *Bull NY Acad Med* 1984;60:722-731.

Systemic Diseases

LEPTOSPIROSIS
(Weil's disease, canicola fever)

Agent
Leptospira interrogans, which occurs as 170 serovars in 20 serologic groups

Distribution
Worldwide

Epidemiology
Zoonotic *Leptospira* infections are widely distributed around the world. Human disease is somewhat more common in tropical than in temperate countries, and infection occurs in the summer or autumn in temperate regions. Most humans are infected by leptospires in water used for drinking, washing, bathing, or swimming. The most common sources of the organisms in the water are chronically infected rats and other rodents, cattle, horses, swine, and dogs that excrete leptospires in urine but are asymptomatic. Numerous wild animals and even reptiles and amphibians may be infected. Leptospirosis is an occupational hazard for rice and sugar cane field workers, military personnel during field exercises, people who swim in contaminated ponds or streams, farmers, veterinarians, and sewer and abattoir workers. In tropical rain forests, infected rodents contaminate stream banks as well as the water. Rainstorms raise the level of the water, which washes leptospires into streams and makes swimming particularly hazardous.

Clinical characteristics and course
After an incubation period of 4 to 19 days, onset is gradual with fever; chills; headache; malaise; myalgia; conjunctival injection; and nausea, vomiting and diarrhea. A small proportion of patients have any or all of the following: aseptic meningitis, rash, uveitis, jaundice, renal failure, hemolytic anemia, or hemorrhagic manifestations. Renal failure, liver changes, and myocarditis could cause death. Infections are more severe in the elderly than in other age groups. Some people exposed to infected animals have subclinical infections.

Diagnosis
Rising antibody titers determined in paired sera with complement fixation, febrile agglutinins, or agglutination tests or an ELISA may demonstrate that a patient with the signs and symptoms listed above has leptospirosis. Leptospires may be isolated by inoculating guinea pigs, hamsters, or gerbils with urine, blood, or tissue suspensions and identifying organisms in the animals' blood with specific antisera. Leptospires may also be cultured.

Principles of treatment
Patients can be treated early with antibiotics.

Prevention
No practical means of prophylaxis exists for travelers. Leptospirocidal antibiotics administered to individuals exposed during the incubation period will prevent disease.

Selected reading
Berman SJ, Tsai CC, Holmes K, et al: Sporadic anicteric leptospirosis in South Vietnam. A study of 150 patients. *Ann Intern Med* 1973;79:167-173.

Elliot DL, Tolle SW, Goldberg L, et al: Pet-associated illness. *N Engl J Med* 1985;313:985-995.

Kennedy ND, Pusey CD, Rainford DJ, et al: Leptospirosis and acute renal failure. Clinical experiences and a review of the literature. *Postgrad Med J* 1979;55:176-179.

MALARIA

Agents
Plasmodium falciparum, Plasmodium vivax, Plasmodium ovale, and *Plasmodium malariae*

Distribution
See Figure 16.

Epidemiology
Malaria can be transmitted by mosquitoes or with a blood transfusion or hypodermic syringe. Female anopheline mosquitoes that feed at various times from dusk to early evening, midnight, or early morning inject the infective sporozoite *Plasmodium* forms. They multiply in the liver cells and become hepatic schizonts that rupture and release merozoites into the bloodstream. They invade the erythrocytes and change from the early ring form through different stages, the last of which is the schizont. It ruptures to release

Systemic Diseases

Figure 16. The distribution of malaria.

Systemic Diseases

multiple infective merozoites that establish serial infections of red blood cells. This occurs nearly every 48 hours during infections with P vivax, P falciparum, and P ovale and every 72 hours during P malariae infections. After several of these cycles, some merozoites change into male and female gametocytes, which, when taken up by mosquitoes, complete the life cycle. The fertilized zygotes multiply into large numbers of infective sporozoites that migrate to the mosquito's salivary glands.

Some P vivax and P ovale organisms may remain dormant in the liver cells and later cause relapses. P malariae may persist for many years as a low-level parasitemia. P falciparum, which causes the most lethal form of the infection, does not have a dormant phase.

Malaria, once prevalent throughout the world, has now been eradicated from the United States, most of Europe, Japan, and Australia and controlled in most large cities. However, malaria continues to be highly prevalent in rural Africa, Latin America, and Asia. P falciparum is the major cause of malaria in Africa. West Africans resist P vivax infections, but P ovale infections are prevalent. Chloroquine-resistant P falciparum, which was first discovered in Colombia in 1961, has now appeared in many parts of the world, especially in Southeast Asia and East Africa.

Clinical characteristics and course

Malaria begins abruptly after an incubation period that differs from one Plasmodium species to another; is reported in various sources as 6 to 30 days; and depends on the parasite strain, host immunity, and prophylactic drugs taken.

The most serious form of malaria is caused by P falciparum; fatality rates may be as high as 20% to 30%. The classic symptoms of malaria are fever, chills, sweats, and headache. Episodes begin with violent shaking, followed by a substantial rise in temperature, and then profuse sweating. At onset, fever may be continuous or irregular. Then febrile paroxysms may become periodic and coincide with release of merozoites. In patients with P ovale and P vivax, the intervals are 48 hours, and in patients with P malariae, the intervals are 72 hours. In patients with P falciparum, intervals are usually quite irregular.

Malaria does not always follow the course described above. In some patients, onset is insidious with low-grade fever; and others have no fever but they do have such symptoms as diarrhea, abdominal pain, dyspnea, headache, or myalgia. Most patients have splenomegaly but not lymphadenopathy.

Patients with P vivax or P ovale may suffer relapses with episodes of recurrent fever for months or years, but patients with P falciparum seldom experience relapses. In nonimmune patients P falciparum malaria can rapidly cause parasitemia in more than half of the red blood cells. This causes a grave emergency characterized by severe hemolysis, jaundice, anemia, acute renal failure, and massive hemoglobinuria. Cerebral malaria, which is more serious, is associated with disorientation, delirium, coma, and high mortality. Chronic, asymptomatic P malariae infection has been associated with the nephrotic syndrome.

Diagnosis

Prompt diagnosis and treatment are essential even in patients with mild malaria because irreversible complications may occur suddenly. Suspect malaria in patients with recurrent fevers and chills, splenomegaly, and anemia. Determine where the patient has been. If the patient has the symptoms and signs described and could have been exposed to malaria, a blood sample should be taken and thick smears prepared. Stain the slides with Giemsa stain, and examine them carefully for parasites. An expert should identify the Plasmodium species in a thin smear. Smears may have to be made at different times of day because parasitemia may be intermittent.

Principles of treatment

Standard treatment of P vivax, P malariae, P ovale, and P falciparum malaria is oral administration of antimalarial chemotherapy. For patients with grave infections, intravenous agents may be used. In the United States, physicians who want to use intravenous agents should telephone the malaria branch of the Centers for Disease Control at 404-452-4046 weekdays or 404-329-2888 evenings, weekends, or holidays.

In extremely severe P falciparum infections with parasitemias approaching 50%, consider exchange transfusions. For drug-resistant P falciparum infections, antimalarial chemotherapy combinations given concurrently or sequentially have been used. Specific drug therapy will usually prevent relapses in patients with P vivax or P ovale infection.

Systemic Diseases

Prevention

Large-scale prevention depends on two strategies: elimination of mosquitoes or prevention of mosquito bites and chemoprophylaxis. Where malaria is prevalent, travelers may wear protective clothing and use mosquito repellents. When staying overnight in buildings that are not air-conditioned, travelers should sleep under mosquito nets. Lowering the temperature with air conditioning not only eliminates the need to open windows but also reduces the biting activity of whatever mosquitoes get inside a building. The nets should be larger than the bed because mosquitoes could bite any part of the body that touches the net. Spraying sleeping quarters with knock-down sprays is useful. Prophylactic agents can be used to suppress or prevent malaria in people who are not immune and who are traveling in areas with no chloroquine-resistant *P falciparum*.

Travelers should be told that no prophylactic regimen unfailingly prevents malaria. They should know the symptoms of malaria, report them to a physician as soon as possible, and not assume that the symptoms are those of another illness. In 1985 the CDC issued specific, detailed recommendations for chemoprophylaxis. Some forms of malaria chemoprophylaxis pose hazards for pregnant women, children less than 2 years old, and patients with G-6-PD deficiency.

Publications from the Centers for Disease Control in Atlanta, Georgia, and the World Health Organization in Geneva, Switzerland, report where malaria is endemic and where the *Plasmodium* organisms are resistant to drugs. Periodically, the two organizations publish updated recommendations for malaria chemoprophylaxis.

Selected reading

Bruce-Chwatt LJ: *Essential Malariology.* London, William Heinemann Medical Books, 1980.

Deans JA, Cohen S: Immunology of malaria. *Annu Rev Microbiol* 1983; 37:25-49.

Miller LH, David PH, Hadley TJ: Perspectives for malaria vaccination. *Philos Trans R Soc Lond Biol* 1984;307:99-115.

Plasmodium vivax infection among tourists to Puerto Vallarta and Acapulco, Mexico, New Mexico, Texas. *MMWR* 1985;34:461-462.

Randall G, Seidel JS: Malaria. *Pediatr Clin North Am* 1985;32:893-916.

Revised recommendations for preventing malaria in travelers to areas with chloroquine-resistant *Plasmodium falciparum* (CRPF). Advisory Memorandum No. 80. Department of Health and Human Services, Atlanta, Georgia, 1985.

Wyler DJ: Malaria – resurgence, resistance, and research. *N Engl J Med* 1983;308:875-878, 934-940.

PLAGUE
(Peste)

Agent
Yersinia pestis

Distribution
See Figure 17.

Epidemiology
Plague is almost exclusively a zoonotic infection. Circumscribed populations of infected rats live in both rural and urban settings throughout the world, especially in Southeast and Central Asia, the Middle East, most of Africa, parts of South America, and in the western United States. Infected rodent fleas, especially *Xenopsylla cheopis*, bite humans and regurgitate *Yersinia* bacteria into the wound, or the bacteria move to humans from infected animal tissue found in rural areas. The prevalence of human infections increases when urban rats are infected by rural fleas. The bacteria can also be transmitted directly from the respiratory tract of one human with untreated septicemic plague or pneumonic plague to the respiratory tract of another who gets pneumonic plague. Near the Andes Mountains, the *Pulex irritans* flea that lives on humans can transmit plague from one human to another.

Clinical characteristics and course
After an incubation period of 2 to 6 days, patients with plague notice fever and swelling of the lymph nodes that drain the site where *Yersinia* bacilli entered the body. The nodes, called *bubos*, (Figure 18) are inflamed and tender and tend to suppurate and to become fluctuant. Bubos occur most commonly in the inguinal region and less commonly near the axilla or on the neck. If not treated, infection may progress to septicemia with metastatic infection of any

Systemic Diseases

Figure 17. The distribution of plague.

Systemic Diseases

Figure 18. A bubo caused by plague. (The overlying skin had been cleaned with iodine in preparation for aspiration.)

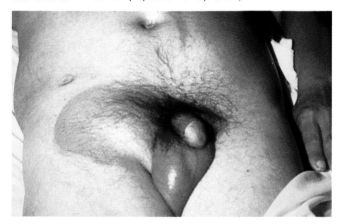

organ, but especially the lung (pneumonic plague) or meninges. Many such infections are fatal.

Diagnosis

The ovoid, bipolar, gram-negative bacilli are easily visible in material aspirated from a bubo, sputum, or cerebrospinal fluid (CSF). A fluorescent antibody test or an antigen-capture ELISA identifies the organism rapidly. Diagnosis is also established by recovery of the organism from lymph, blood, sputum, or cerebrospinal fluid. With a passive hemagglutination test, a rise in specific antibody titers can be demonstrated in paired sera.

Principles of treatment

Fluids of bubonic plague patients should be handled carefully for 72 hours. Several antibiotics are effective if therapy begins within 24 hours after onset. In some patients with septicemic or pneumonic plague, therapy must begin soon after infection to prevent death. Suppurative bubos may need to be incised and drained if fever recurs.

Prevention

Two or three doses of plague vaccine usually provide protection. Antibiotics can be given prophylactically.

Selected reading

Christie AB: Plague: Review of ecology. *Ecol Dis* 1982;1:111-115.

RELAPSING FEVER

Agent
Borrelia recurrentis and at least 15 other *Borrelia* species

Distribution
See Figure 19.

Epidemiology
Relapsing fever is called epidemic when spread by lice and endemic when spread by ticks. Louse-borne relapsing fever occurs in limited areas of Asia, Ethiopia, the Sudan, northern and Central Africa, and the Andean region of South America and is usually associated with catastrophic events. Infection results from crushing an infected louse over a wound or on an abrasion and not from injection of louse saliva or excrement. Epidemic disease is transmitted by *Pediculus humanus* lice, which remain infected for life after feeding on infected blood.

Tick-borne relapsing fever is endemic in tropical Africa with foci in Spain, northern Africa, Saudi Arabia, Iran, India, Central Asia, and parts of North and South America. The organism circulates in wild rodents and other small animals and is ingested by the ticks as they bite the animals. The organism is also transmitted from one generation of ticks to another in the ovaries. Humans are infected as ticks feed, usually at night.

Clinical characteristics and course
Clinically the two forms of relapsing fever are similar. After an incubation period of 5 to 15 days, relapsing fever begins abruptly, lasts for 2 to 9 days, and is followed by an afebrile period of 2 to 4 days. Rigors, severe headache, myalgias, lethargy, photophobia, and cough usually accompany the fever. Initially patients may also have conjunctival suffusion, petechiae, diffuse abdominal tenderness, enlarged liver and spleen, and mild hemorrhages. Some patients have neurologic signs and symptoms. Louse-borne infections tend to relapse only once, and tick-borne infections relapse repeatedly. Fatality rates in untreated patients may be 10% or higher.

Diagnosis
Demonstration of the spirochete in darkfield preparations of fresh blood or blood smears suggests that the disease is

Systemic Diseases

Figure 19. The distribution of relapsing fever.

Systemic Diseases

probably relapsing fever. Diagnosis is confirmed by recovery of the organism from the blood of laboratory mice or rats that have received intraperitoneal inoculations of blood from the patient.

Principles of treatment

Several antibiotics can cure the infection. Following treatment, most patients with louse-borne and some patients with tick-borne infections suffer Jarisch-Herxheimer reactions. Medical personnel should anticipate the reactions and prepare to treat them.

Prevention

The infection can best be prevented by the eradication with insecticides of the human body louse and argasid ticks. Good personal hygiene is the best protection against lice. Tick bites can be prevented by wearing tight-fitting, long-sleeved shirts and long pants tucked into boots and by using tick repellents.

Selected reading

Bryceson ADN, Parry EHO, Perrine PL, et al: Louse-bourne relapsing fever. A clinical and laboratory study of 62 cases in Ethiopia and a reconsideration of the literature. *Q J Med* 1970;39:129-170.

Burgdorfer W: The diagnosis of relapsing fever, in Johnson RC (ed): *The Biology of Parasitic Spirochetes.* New York, Academic Press, 1976, pp 225-232.

Gear JH: The hemorrhagic fevers of Southern Africa with special reference to studies in the South Africa Institute for Medical Research. *Yale J Biol Med* 1982;55:207-212.

Goubau PF: Relapsing fevers. A review. *Ann Soc Belg Med Trop* 1984; 64:335-364.

SCHISTOSOMIASIS
(Bilharziasis, snail fever)

Agents
Schistosoma mansoni, Schistosoma intercalatum, Schistosoma japonicum, Schistosoma mekongi, Schistosoma haematobium

Distribution
See Figures 20 and 21.

Epidemiology
Three species of blood flukes are important causes of schistosomiasis. The final habitats of the flukes are the venules of the intestines (S mansoni and S japonicum) or urinary bladder (S haematobium) and the liver, lungs, ureters, and the central nervous system. S mekongi and S intercalatum occasionally infect humans.

As with other fluke infections, the snail is the intermediate host for the schistosomes. The snails that carry both S mansoni and S haematobium are aquatic, and the snails that carry S japonicum are amphibious. When snails are infected with miracidia, ciliated free-swimming organisms that hatch from schistosome eggs deposited in fresh water, asexual reproduction takes place and hundreds or thousands of cercariae are produced and released into the water.

These free-swimming cercariae penetrate directly through human skin. The young schistosomes migrate to the lungs and then to the portal venous system of the liver, where they mature and mate. Then they pass into the mesenteric or bladder venules, and adult schistosomes attach to blood vessel walls with suckers. With the help of proteolytic enzymes, eggs pass out of blood vessels, penetrate tissues, and enter the lumen of the gut or the urinary bladder, from which they are excreted. The life-span of the schistosome usually averages between 3 and 5 years although some have survived longer.

Schistosomes multiply abundantly in the snail intermediate host, which dies as a result; but they do not multiply in humans. S mansoni flukes live in Arabia, Africa, South America, and the Caribbean; S haematobium in Africa and the Middle East; and S japonicum in Japan, China, Sulawesi, the Philippines, Thailand, Laos, and Kampuchea. The density of infective cercariae in most bodies of fresh water is low because few snails are infected and because cercariae are dispersed in large volumes of water. People briefly in contaminated water rarely become significantly infected. A small proportion of people in areas where schistosomiasis is endemic are exposed to high densities of cercariae, and those people may be infected with large numbers of worms.

Clinical characteristics and course
Mild infections have few clinical consequences; disease appears to be associated with intensity of infection and is due to the deposition of large numbers of parasite eggs in the

Systemic Diseases

Figure 20. Distribution of schistosomiasis caused by *S haematobium* and *S japonicum*.

●●●● *S haematobium*
●●●● *S japonicum*

Systemic Diseases

host tissues. Schistosomiasis may cause three different syndromes: schistosome dermatitis immediately following penetration of cercariae; acute schistosomiasis, which begins several weeks after exposure; and chronic schistosomiasis, which takes many years to develop.

Dermatitis. Although dermatitis (swimmer's itch) (Figure 22) has occurred in patients infected with the three most important human schistosomes, the dermatitis is more common in patients infected with avian or other animal schistosomes that die within the skin. A pruritic maculopapular rash that may be followed by erythema, vesicle formation, and edema develops only in people exposed repeatedly to cercariae in water. This reaction appears to be an immunologic response with both immediate and delayed components. Schistosome dermatitis occurs throughout the world.

Acute schistosomiasis. In contrast, acute schistosomiasis, also known as Katayama fever, seems to occur only during primary infection in people exposed to high concentrations of cercariae; and the pathogenesis may resemble that of antigen-antibody-complex-mediated serum sickness. Fever begins 3 to 8 weeks after exposure and may last for several weeks. Fever appears most commonly in patients infected with S japonicum, much less commonly in patients infected with S mansoni, and rarely in patients infected with S haematobium. Patients also have chills, sweating, headache, hepatosplenomegaly, lymphadenopathy, eosinophilia, and a cough. In patients with large numbers of S japonicum worms, Katayama fever can cause severe illness and death.

Chronic hepatosplenic schistosomiasis. An immune response to schistosome eggs trapped in the tissues causes the signs and symptoms of chronic schistosomiasis. The eggs elicit a delayed-hypersensitivity granulomatous reaction that destroys tissue and produces fibrosis. The eggs themselves do not significantly obstruct blood flow; the granulomatous and fibrotic tissue formed produces portal hypertension and esophageal varices.

The earliest sign of chronic schistosomiasis is hepatomegaly followed by splenomegaly. The results of liver function tests are usually normal, and most patients do not suffer the problems associated with chronic liver disease.

The most important complication of hepatosplenic schistosomiasis is hematemesis due to ruptured esophageal varices. However, the mortality rate is low because patients whose liver function is normal do not experience hepatic coma. Patients may also have signs and symptoms of liver parenchymal disease, but whether it is a natural progression of the schistosomiasis or related to other diseases such as hepatitis B is not known.

Chronic schistosomiasis can also cause pulmonary hypertension and cor pulmonale because eggs lodge in the pulmonary arterioles and cause granulomas to form. Chronic schistosomiasis rarely affects the central nervous system. However, ectopic S japonicum worm pairs lay large masses of eggs in the brain, and they produce focal epilepsy or diffuse cerebral disease. S mansoni and S haematobium are found more often in the spinal cord than in the brain and are associated with a transverse myelitis-like syndrome.

Chronic genitourinary schistosomiasis. In patients with severe, long-term S haematobium infections, granulomas formed in the bladder wall obstruct urine flow at the bladder entrance. This may cause hydronephrosis and uremia. Reduced distensibility of the bladder because of fibrotic calcification may cause urinary frequency and dysuria. Cancer of the bladder is a complication of S haematobium infection.

Diagnosis

A crucial factor in the diagnosis of schistosomiasis is a history of significant contact with fresh water. No one is infected with schistosomes while swimming in chlorinated swimming pools or in the ocean. Definite diagnosis is made by finding schistosome eggs in the urine or feces.

For S mansoni and S japonicum infections, the Kato thick smear is the procedure of choice. A 50 mL sample of feces is pressed through 105-mesh stainless steel bolting cloth, placed on a glass slide, and covered with a cellophane cover slip impregnated with 50% glycerine. The slides are inverted and pressed onto a bed of filter paper, inverted again, and left for 24 hours while the fecal matter clears. Then the eggs in the sample are counted and multiplied by 20, which provides the number of eggs per gram of feces.

To diagnose S haematobium infections, eggs can easily be detected by scanning the sediment of a urine sample collected in the middle of the day and lightly centrifuged. For determining intensity, a 10 mL aliquot of urine may be passed through a membrane filter. The filter is removed from the chamber, placed face down on a microscope slide, and examined immediately at 40 times magnification. In patients with hepatosplenic schistosomiasis and normal func-

Systemic Diseases

Figure 21. Distribution of schistosomiasis caused by *S intercalatum* and *S mansoni*.

•••• *S intercalatum*
•••• *S mansoni*

Systemic Diseases

Figure 22. Diffuse papules of swimmer's itch.

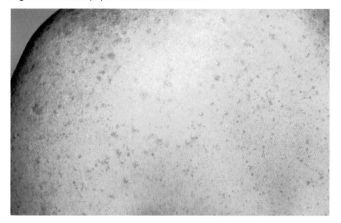

tion of the liver parenchyma, the portal system collateral circulation may be documented by splenoportography. Chronic *S haematobium* infection can be diagnosed with intravenous or retrograde pyelography or cystoscopy.

Principles of treatment
Anthelmintic therapy is effective in treating the forms of schistosomiasis caused by adult egg-producing worms. In patients with hepatosplenic disease, conservative treatment is best. Only after repeated episodes of bleeding should surgery be done. Some patients with *S haematobium* infections will need to have the patency of the bladder outlet restored surgically.

Prevention
Travelers should be extremely cautious about swimming in ponds, lakes, or streams and about sanitary disposal of human waste in countries where schistosomes are endemic. People who must go into contaminated water should wear rubber boots and gloves to minimize cercarial penetration, towel dry wet skin vigorously, and immediately wash skin that has been immersed in contaminated water with 70% alcohol.

Selected reading

Akpom CA: Schistosomiasis: Nutritional implications. *Rev Infect Dis* 1982; 4:776-782.

Archer S: The chemotherapy of schistosomiasis. *Annu Rev Pharmacol Toxicol* 1985;25:485-508.

Davis A: Recent advances in schistosomiasis. *Q J Med* 1986;58:95-110.

DeCock KM: Hepatosplenic schistosomiasis: A clinical review. *Gut* 1986; 27:734-745.

Scrimgeour EM, Gajdusek DC: Involvement of the central nervous system in *Schistosoma mansoni* and *S haematobium* infection. A review. *Brain* 1985; 108:1023-1038.

Warren KS: Regulation of the prevalence and intensity of schistosomiasis in man: Immunology or ecology? *J Infect Dis* 1973;127:595-609.

TRYPANOSOMIASIS, AFRICAN
(African sleeping sickness)

Agents
Trypanosoma brucei gambiense, Trypanosoma brucei rhodesiense

Distribution
See Figure 23.

Epidemiology
Infection with *T gambiense* causes classic African sleeping sickness, and infection with *T rhodesiense* causes a more acute form of trypanosomiasis. Trypanosomes disseminate into the peripheral blood and lymph nodes 1 to 3 weeks after inoculation into humans. The organisms enter the cerebrospinal fluid of patients with the Rhodesian infection more quickly than they enter the cerebrospinal fluid of patients with the Gambian infection.

Tsetse flies transmit both forms of African trypanosomiasis. The species of the *Glossina* tsetse fly vector varies with the trypanosome. Both male and female flies bite, but infective forms have been found in less than 10% of flies fed trypanosomes.

Trypanosomiasis transmission occurs between 15 degrees north and 15 degrees south latitude in Africa. *T rhodesiense* lives mainly in the eastern third of Central Africa, and *T gambiense* lives mainly in the western half of Central Africa. The flies that transmit the Rhodesian disease live in vast, sparsely inhabited areas of the East African plains, and they have been found on several different species of game animals. The flies that transmit Gambian trypanosomiasis live along the forested banks of rivers and in other similarly humid areas. They usually transmit the disease when humans cross the river or work or play in it.

Systemic Diseases

Figure 23. The distribution of African trypanosomiasis and American trypanosomiasis.

●●●●*T brucei gambiense*
●●●●*T brucei rhodesiense*
●●●●*T brucei gambiense and rhodesiense*
●●●●*T cruzi*

Systemic Diseases

Humans, dogs, and pigs can host the parasite.

Clinical characteristics and course

A trypanosomal chancre may appear 2 or 3 days after a tsetse fly has bitten the patient. In 4 to 10 days the chancre becomes a small, hard, painful red nodule surrounded by a zone of erythema and swelling 3 to 4 inches in diameter. The lesions, usually accompanied by regional lymphadenopathy, are generally on the head or the leg. They disappear completely within 2 weeks when the trypanosomes invade the bloodstream and systemic signs and symptoms appear. They include fever, headache, and at times, shaking chills. Lymphadenopathy becomes generalized. About 2 months after the onset of the illness, Caucasians may notice a large, erythematous circinate patchy rash on the skin. Blacks do not notice the lesion. Nonspecific neurologic symptoms include headache, insomnia, and delayed pain sensation. Clinical laboratory test results show anemia, monocytosis, and very high concentrations of serum IgM.

Rhodesian trypanosomes invade the central nervous system 3 to 6 weeks after the fly bites and cause constant headache and recurrent fever and weakness. Most patients have tachycardia; and if the patient dies at this stage, myocarditis is usually the cause. Survivors may become irritable and may have insomnia and personality and mood changes accompanied by weakness, anemia, and peripheral edema. Untreated patients die within 6 to 9 months usually from secondary infection or cardiac failure.

Gambian trypanosomiasis may not cause the typical signs and symptoms of sleeping sickness for months or years after the patient is bitten. Fever and lymphadenopathy are the early signs of infection. Invasion of the central nervous system causes meningoencephalomyelitis predominantly in the base of the brain. Drowsiness, indifference, and an uncontrollable urge to sleep characterize the infection. Behavioral changes, tremors, rigidity, and ataxia are common. Before treatment was available, Gambian trypanosomiasis was always fatal.

Diagnosis

Suspect African trypanosomiasis in patients who have traveled in the countries where the infection is endemic and who have a skin nodule, fever, lymphadenopathy, circinate rash, or emotional changes. People who have been only in large cities are highly unlikely to have the infection. The bite of the tsetse fly is memorable. The fly is about one-half inch long and brown to gray, and the bite is painful.

To make a specific diagnosis, examine aspirate from an enlarged lymph node or a thick blood smear made from red cells concentrated by centrifugation. If the patient has central nervous system disease, withdraw a sample of cerebrospinal fluid, centrifuge, and examine the sediment for trypomastigotes. An ELISA or agglutination tests will demonstrate specific antibodies. Concentrations of immunoglobulins, especially IgM, are elevated.

Principles of treatment

Investigational drugs are available from the Centers for Disease Control.

Prevention

Travelers should avoid the habitats of the tsetse fly and should use repellents and insecticides. People who live where Gambian trypanosomes are indigenous should be regularly surveyed for infection and the infections treated.

Selected reading

Askonas BA, Bancroft GJ: Interaction of African trypanosomes with the immune system. *Philos Trans R Soc Lond Biol* 1984;307:41-49.

Foulkes JR: Human trypanosomiasis in Africa. *Br Med J* 1981;283: 1172-1174.

Greenwood BM, Whittle HC: The pathogenesis of sleeping sickness. *Trans R Soc Trop Med Hyg* 1980;74:716-725.

VanMeirvenne N, LeRay D: Diagnosis of African and American trypanosomiases. *Br Med Bull* 1985;41:156-161.

Vickerman K: Development cycles and biology of pathogenic trypanosomes. *Br Med Bull* 1985;41:105-114.

TRYPANOSOMIASIS, AMERICAN
(Chagas' disease)

Agent
Trypanosoma cruzi

Distribution
See Figure 23.

Systemic Diseases

Epidemiology

American trypanosomiasis occurs only in the Western Hemisphere, where it is known as Chagas' disease. Large bloodsucking insects known as reduviid bugs transmit the infection.

In passage from the insect to vertebrate hosts, T cruzi organisms undergo major morphologic changes. As the insects bite, they defecate the infective forms; and the feces are either brushed into the bite or directly contaminate the conjunctivae, mucous membranes, or abrasions. After several weeks, the organisms penetrate the cells of the reticuloendothelial system and striated and cardiac muscle of the host. The parasites multiply by binary fission; and some revert to an earlier form and reenter the bloodstream, from which reduviid bugs can ingest them.

American trypanosomiasis occurs chiefly in rural Mexico and Central and South America, where people live in adobe, mud, or cane huts. Cracks in the walls or thatched roofs provide a place for reduviid bugs to live and breed. Other reasons why the infection is so prevalent in those places are the animal reservoirs of the parasite, the degree of adaptation of the insect vectors to support parasite growth, and the virulence of various parasite strains. Natural infection with T cruzi occurs in species that are widespread in the Western Hemisphere, and they include opossums, raccoons, and armadillos in the United States. In various parts of the hemisphere, the infection rate in reduviid bugs is estimated to be 20% to 60%. The parasite can also be transmitted by blood transfusion, across the placenta, and in human milk.

Clinical characteristics and course

Most infected people have no symptoms in the early stages of the infection, but acute infections may occur 5 to 14 days after the reduviid bug has bitten. One quarter of the acutely ill patients do not react at the site of entry of the trypanosomes; in one quarter a nodular lesion, the chagoma, appears; and in half the classical facial lesion, the Romaña's sign, caused by unilateral, painless, palpebral swelling develops. In patients with either lesion, the lymph nodes draining the site of the lesion enlarge. As the parasite moves through the bloodstream, a small proportion of patients may have malaise, fever, muscle pain, nontender lymphadenopathy, and hepatosplenomegaly. Those patients may also have tachycardia and arrhythmias. Mortality in patients with acute trypanosomiasis is about 10%.

Chronic trypanosomiasis may develop in about 10% of patients who had acute Chagas' disease and in asymptomatic patients. Destruction of the autonomic ganglia and myositis or both cause chronic disease. As a result the heart, esophagus, colon, bronchi, and other hollow structures are denervated. The mechanism of destruction of the nerve cells is not known, but an immune reaction may cause the myositis.

Cardiomyopathy is the most common result of Chagas' disease. At first the patient appears to have congestive heart failure. The heart enlarges, and in 70% of patients cardiac conduction is disturbed, usually by right bundle branch block. The esophagus and colon may enlarge and dilate substantially, a condition called megadisease. Patients with megaesophagus usually have dysphagia and regurgitation, and patients with megacolon usually have constipation. The prevalence of megadisease varies from one area to another.

Diagnosis

A history of reduviid bug bites, fever, lymphadenopathy, or congestive heart failure or symptoms of megadisease suggest that a patient may have Chagas' disease. The patient would have lived in native housing in a rural area where the disease is endemic. To diagnose acute illness, examine blood smears stained with Giemsa stain for C-shaped stained organisms and unstained smears for mobile trypanosomes. Centrifuging heparinized blood will concentrate the organisms. Organisms can also be cultured, injected intraperitoneally into mice and recovered, or identified by a process known as xenodiagnosis, in which uninfected triatomid bugs are fed on the patient's blood and the bug's feces are examined for parasites 1 to 2 months later. To diagnose chronic Chagas' disease, you must use xenodiagnosis or serologic tests.

Principles of treatment

No treatment is known for T cruzi infection although certain experimental drugs are being studied. Two such drugs are available from the CDC. Chronic myocarditis can be treated symptomatically, and megadisease can be treated with diet or surgical procedures.

Prevention

Application of residual insecticides in and around houses,

Systemic Diseases

the use of mosquito nets, and repair of the cracks where the reduviid bugs live are the most important means for preventing Chagas' disease.

Selected reading

Hudson L, Britten V: Immune response to South American trypanosomiasis and its relationship to Chagas' disease. *Br Med Bull* 1985; 41:162-168.

Marsden P: Selective primary health care: Strategies for the control of disease in the developing world. XVI. Chagas' disease. *Rev Infect Dis* 1984; 6:855-865.

Miles MA: The epidemiology of South American trypanosomiasis – Biochemical and immunological approaches and their relevance to control. *Trans R Soc Trop Med Hyg* 1983; 77:2-23.

VanMeirvenne N, LeRay D: Diagnosis of African and American trypanosomiases. *Br Med Bull* 1985; 41:156-161.

Vickerman K: Development cycles and biology of pathogenic trypanosomes. *Br Med Bull* 1985; 41:105-114.

TYPHOID FEVER AND PARATYPHOID FEVER

Agents
Salmonella typhi, 106 types identified by phage typing; *Salmonella paratyphi* types A, B, and C

Distribution
Worldwide

Epidemiology
Organisms from carriers or recently infected people contaminate water, shellfish, raw fruit, vegetables, milk, and milk products. The contamination is direct through food handling or indirect from fecal contamination of waste water. S typhi or S paratyphi may multiply in food at ambient temperature to reach infective thresholds. An estimated 10% of untreated patients will discharge bacilli for 3 months after infection, and 2% to 5% of infected patients become carriers. Most are middle-aged women who harbor organisms in gallstones in infected gallbladders. *Schistosoma haematobium* infections of the urinary bladder and stone formation predispose people to excrete typhoid bacilli chronically.

Clinical characteristics and course
For both typhoid and paratyphoid fevers, the incubation period depends on the inoculum, ranges from 1 to 3 weeks, and is followed by insidious onset of fever, headache, malaise, anorexia, abdominal pain, splenomegaly, bradycardia, rose spots on the skin of the trunk, and constipation. Diarrhea occurs later. Subsequently, the courses of typhoid and paratyphoid fevers differ. In patients with untreated typhoid fever, fever continues to increase, and the patient may become stuporous. Ulceration of Peyer's patches in the ileum may produce hemorrhage or perforation. Leukopenia and anemia are common. The fatality rate in untreated people is at least 10%.

The symptoms and signs of paratyphoid fever resemble those of typhoid fever, but they are consistently less severe. The mortality rate in patients with paratyphoid fever is negligible.

Diagnosis
Salmonella organisms can be isolated from blood, urine, or feces. Bone marrow is an excellent source. The diseases can be diagnosed serologically in patients who have not been vaccinated when antibody titers rise as measured by a Widal's serum agglutination test using H and O antigens. Increased O titers are more specific than increased H titers.

Principles of treatment
Antibiotics have been effective treatment for patients with typhoid or paratyphoid fever, but antibiotic treatment prolongs the excretion of the organisms in the stool. Relapses occur in some treated patients. They can be treated again with the same or different antibiotics. Until stool cultures are negative, stools should be handled carefully and the organisms destroyed before disposal. Antibiotics do not always eliminate organisms from persistent carriers, especially if the carrier has gallbladder disease. Cholescystectomy followed by antibiotic treatment for 6 weeks may be necessary.

Prevention
Fly control, sanitary disposal of fecal waste, and pasteurization of milk are the first principles of control. Carriers must

Systemic Diseases

be identified and prevented from working in food preparation. Precautions in handling the stools of patients and careful handwashing by nurses prevent the spread of typhoid fever. In community trials, an oral, live, attenuated vaccine has given good protection.

Selected reading

Bitar R, Tarpley J: Intestinal perforation in typhoid fever: A historical and state-of-the-art review. *Rev Infect Dis* 1985;7:257-271.

Levine MM, Kaper JB, Black RE, et al: New knowledge on pathogenesis of bacterial enteric infections as applied to vaccine development. *Microbiol Rev* 1983;47:510-550.

Hook EW: Typhoid fever today. *N Engl J Med* 1984; 310:116-118.

Mandal BK: Typhoid and paratyphoid fever. *Clin Gasteroenterol* 1979; 8:715-735.

Taylor DN, Pollard RA, Blake PA: Typhoid fever in the United States and the risk to the international traveler. *J Infect Dis* 1983;148:599-602.

Warren JW, Hornick RB: Immunization against typhoid fever. *Annu Rev Med* 1979; 30:457-472.

TYPHUS FEVERS: LOUSE-BORNE TYPHUS, MURINE TYPHUS, AND SCRUB TYPHUS

Agents
Rickettsia prowazekii (louse-borne typhus), *Rickettsia typhi* (murine typhus), and *Rickettsia tsutsugamushi* (scrub typhus)

Distribution
See Figure 24.

Epidemiology
Louse-borne typhus. In the past the disease was associated with wars and human disasters. Now the disease is endemic in mountainous regions of Mexico and Asia, in Central and South America, and in Central Africa. The human body louse *Pediculus humanus* is infected when it feeds on infected blood. The louse excretes the organisms as it feeds on a second host, and they are rubbed into the bite wound or inoculated through scratch abrasions. The infected lice die; humans are the reservoir.

Murine typhus. Infected rats and a rat flea vector, *Xenopsylla cheopis*, harbor the *R typhi* responsible for murine typhus. In human habitats or workplaces infested with rats, rat fleas transmit the organism to man just as the human body louse transmits *R prowazekii*.

Scrub typhus. *R tsutsugamushi* organisms are passed from adult trombiculid mites such as *Leptotrombidium akamushi* to eggs in the mite ovary. The infected larval mite transmits the rickettsiae to man and to rodents, which are the reservoirs but not part of the rickettsiae's life cycle. The mites, rodents, and rickettsiae live in small areas of scrub growth throughout the Soviet Far East, Japan, China, Southeast Asia, northern Australia, India, and parts of Pakistan. Scrub typhus is a disease of forest workers and gatherers, rubber plantation workers, and military personnel.

Clinical characteristics and course
After an incubation period of 1 to 2 weeks in patients with louse-borne and murine infections and 10 to 12 days in patients with scrub typhus, fever, chills, headache, prostration, conjunctival injection, and myalgia begin abruptly. Louse-borne typhus, the most severe of the three, can produce toxemia, stupor, and a macular rash. In untreated patients, the fatality rate is 10% to 40%. Murine typhus is milder and has a fatality rate of 1% to 2%. In patients with scrub typhus, a punched-out skin ulcer appears at the site of attachment of the infected mite. Lymphadenopathy is common. Fatality rates in patients with scrub typhus vary from 1% to 60% because the virulence of organisms differs substantially. Many patients cough, and their chest x-ray films show pneumonitis. Patients with any of the three infections may have a rash on the trunk and the arms and legs.

Diagnosis
Rickettsiae can be isolated by inoculating patients' blood into mice, eggs, or tissue culture. Serologic diagnosis can be established in paired sera tested with a fluorescent antibody test, complement fixation test, toxin neutralization test, or the Weil-Felix reaction, in which *Proteus X* bacteria are agglutinated. The Weil-Felix reaction is readily available and easy to do but not as reliable as some other tests. Sera from patients with louse-borne typhus agglutinate *Proteus* OX-19, and sera from scrub typhus patients agglutinate *Proteus* OXK.

Systemic Diseases

Figure 24. The distribution of louse-borne and scrub typhus.

●●●● Louse-borne typhus
●●●● Scrub typhus

Systemic Diseases

Principles of treatment

Several antibiotics are effective. They should be administered until the patient is afebrile. Some patients may need intravenous therapy. Recrudescences (Brill's or Brill-Zinsser disease) are common, especially among elderly people, and require additional treatment with the drugs used originally.

Prevention

To prevent transmission of R prowazekii, delouse clothing and fomites. To prevent infection, a vaccine is available to military personnel but is not licensed for general use. To prevent scrub typhus, impregnate clothing with miticides, and apply mite repellents to the skin. Numerous insecticides will eliminate mites from selected areas. Prophylactic antibiotics can be given to people at high risk of infection.

Selected reading

Burnett JW: Rickettsioses: A review for the dermatologist. *J Am Acad Dermatol* 1980; 2:359-373.

Louse-borne typhus 1981-1982. *Weekly Epidemiol Record* 1984; 59:29-30.

Riley HD Jr: Rickettsial diseases and Rocky Mountain spotted fever – Part II. *Curr Probl Pediatr* 1981; 11:1-38.

Woodward TE: Keep murine typhus in mind. *JAMA* 1986; 255:2211-2212.

YELLOW FEVER

Agents

Yellow fever viruses (Togaviridae, *Flavivirus*)

Distribution

See Figure 25.

Epidemiology

Yellow fever has two forms: urban yellow fever transmitted by the *Aedes aegypti* mosquito from one infected human to another human who is not immune and sylvan or jungle yellow fever which normally infects several monkey species but is transmitted to some humans by several species of forest mosquitoes of the genus *Haemagogus*.

In the American hemisphere, urban yellow fever has not been reported in about 40 years; however jungle yellow fever has been reported in humans in South America. The epidemiology in Africa is more complex. Yellow fever is enzootic in a wide belt including West, Central, and East Africa south of the Sahara Desert. Urban yellow fever outbreaks occur frequently within the belt, and major recent outbreaks have occurred in Ethiopia, Burkina Faso, and Senegal. Several species of the subgenus *Stegomyia* transmit the disease. Jungle yellow fever also occurs in humans in Africa.

Clinical characteristics and course

In a large proportion of yellow fever patients, infection causes only mild fever and other signs and symptoms that resemble those of influenza. In the other patients, after an incubation period of 3 to 6 days, onset is acute; but severity varies widely. Fever, chills, headache, backache, and nausea and vomiting are early symptoms. In severe infections, patients suffer prostration, mild bradycardia, jaundice, and albuminuria that may progress to anuria. In patients with severe infections, signs of hemorrhage, such as epistaxis, bleeding gums, hematemesis, and melena, are common. Severe bleeding and marked jaundice connote a grave prognosis. In some outbreaks, fatality has been as high as 50%, but usually fatality ranges from 5% to 10%.

Diagnosis

The virus can be recovered from blood drawn during the acute phase of the infection and inoculated in mice, mosquitoes, or tissue cultures. If the blood must be transported to a laboratory, it should be cooled to 4° C. An antigen-capture ELISA demonstrates viral antigen. Specific IgM antibody can be found in serum drawn during the acute or early convalescent phase, or neutralization or complement fixation tests will demonstrate a rise in antibody titer in paired sera. The hemagglutination inhibition test provides only a presumptive diagnosis because of cross-reactions with other flaviviruses.

Principles of treatment

Treatment is supportive. Replacement of fluid and electrolytes is essential. Blood or platelet transfusions may help to control bleeding.

Systemic Diseases

Figure 25. The distribution of yellow fever.

Prevention

Anyone traveling to countries where yellow fever is enzootic or endemic should be given yellow fever vaccine 17D. Border authorities in many countries with *A aegypti* mosquitoes in urban areas require evidence of valid yellow fever immunization from people arriving from any area with urban or jungle yellow fever.

A aegypti mosquitoes bite in the daytime and breed in and near human habitation. Visitors to marketplaces, schools, hospitals, or homes during daylight hours may risk exposure to the insects. In many tropical countries *A aegypti* breeds in and near hotels and restaurants. People visiting countries where yellow fever is endemic or during an epidemic should apply mosquito repellent to all exposed body surfaces.

Selected reading

Yellow fever in the Americas. *Bull Pan Am Health Organ* 1985;19:209-212.

Other Diseases or Circumstances to Consider in the Differential Diagnosis of Systemic Diseases in Travelers and Immigrants

ACTINOMYCOSIS
BRUCELLOSIS
COCCIDIOIDOMYCOSIS
LYME DISEASE
MELIOIDOSIS
MUMPS
VENOMOUS BITES AND STINGS

Respiratory Diseases

ANTHRAX
(Malignant pustule, malignant edema)

Agent
Bacillus anthracis

Distribution
Worldwide

Epidemiology
In humans, anthrax is endemic in agricultural areas where animal anthrax is common. Anthrax spores, which are highly infectious, may survive in contaminated soil for many years; and the disease spreads among grazing animals through contaminated soil and feed. Human disease is primarily an occupational hazard of workers who process hides; hair, especially goat hair; bone; and wool contaminated with spores. Veterinarians and agricultural workers who handle infected animals are also in danger. The spores pass through wounds or abrasions or enter the skin on an animal hair that has penetrated the skin. People who do not work with animals may contact anthrax spores on animal products such as brushes or infected hides. Humans may also be infected by inhaling spores or by eating undercooked infected meat.

Clinical characteristics and course
The incubation period is less than 1 week, often 2 to 5 days. Anthrax occurs in three forms: cutaneous, pneumonic, and intestinal. In patients with cutaneous anthrax, exposed skin itches, papules appear and then become vesicular, and in 2 to 6 days a black eschar surrounded by erythema and sometimes by secondary vesicles replaces the original lesion (Figures 26 and 27). A scar forms as the lesion heals. In either form, the lesions are painless unless a secondary infection develops. Untreated infections may spread to regional lymph nodes and then to the blood and cause overwhelming septicemia and in some patients, meningitis.

Pneumonic or inhalation anthrax begins as a mild upper respiratory infection and in 3 to 5 days progresses to fever, mediastinal widening, and shock; death follows shortly.

Intestinal anthrax tends to occur in outbreaks among people sharing a meal of undercooked, infected meat. Abdominal distress precedes fever, septicemia, and death. In untreated patients, fatality rates are 50% to 90%.

Figure 26. Malignant pustule of anthrax.

Figure 27. Cutaneous diphtheria which can be mistaken for anthrax.

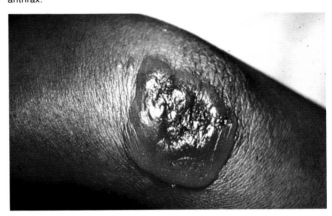

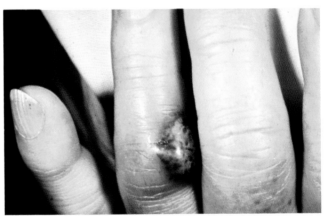

Diagnosis
Gram stain demonstrates *B anthracis* in blood, pus, or scrapings or exudates from lesions. The organism can be recovered in culture medium or in blood of mice, guinea pigs, or rabbits inoculated with the patient's blood or scrapings from lesions. Antibody responses in paired sera can be measured by the fluorescent antibody test, the indirect hemagglutination test, or an ELISA.

Principles of treatment
Several antibiotics cure the infection. The cutaneous form can be treated with oral therapy, but the other forms may require parenteral therapy. Therapy for the other forms is empirical or based on animal data. Drainage and secretion precautions should be followed.

Respiratory Diseases

Prevention

A vaccine is available for people at high risk. For the traveler, prevention consists of not buying materials made from the hides of goats, cattle, sheep, or pigs where those animals transmit anthrax. The World Health Organization and the Centers for Disease Control publish a list of such countries. Because few travelers get advice about buying leather, physicians should be alert to early symptoms of anthrax even though the probability that a traveler will catch the disease is low.

Selected reading

Hambleton P, Carman JA, Melling J: Anthrax: The disease in relation to vaccines. *Vaccine* 1984;2:125-132.

Knudson GB: Treatment of anthrax in man: History and current concepts. *Milit Med* 1986;151:71-77.

PARAGONIMIASIS
(Pulmonary distomiasis, lung fluke disease)

Distribution
See Figure 28.

Agents
Paragonimus westermani and other species in Asia, Africa, and South America

Epidemiology
Paragonimus westermani lung flukes are distributed worldwide, but infection in man is chiefly confined to the Far East although infection has been reported in Africa and South and Central America. Dietary habits are a major factor in the distribution of this infection.

Free-swimming *Paragonimus* cercariae attack various species of freshwater crayfish and crabs and encyst in the tissues as metacercariae. After humans ingest raw or pickled crustacea or unpickled sauces made from the crayfish and crabs, metacercariae excyst in the duodenum, penetrate the intestinal wall, and enter the peritoneal cavity. They migrate into the lungs where they mature into adult flukes that finally lodge near the bronchioles and remain within tissue capsules laid down by the host. The circuitous route of migration through the host's tissues explains the appearance of flukes in ectopic sites, the most important of which is the brain.

The adult flukes produce golden brown eggs that are eventually passed in the feces. After several weeks, free-swimming ciliated miracidia hatch and penetrate into suitable snail species. There the larvae develop into cercariae and then leave the snails to complete the cycle. Humans, dogs, pigs, and wild carnivores are definitive hosts and reservoirs.

Clinical characteristics and course
Intensity of infection is related to how many metacercariae a person has eaten. Most infections are light to moderate and asymptomatic.

Flukes mature and begin to lay eggs approximately 6 weeks after a person ingests metacercariae. The onset of symptoms varies, and the primary symptoms are eosinophilia and cough. The patient may also report intermittent hemoptysis, profuse expectoration, and pleuritic chest pain. Moist, coarse rales over the infection site are prominent characteristics. Cerebral paragonimiasis occurs in regions where large numbers of *Paragonimus* organisms are endemic and usually after the onset of pulmonary symptoms. The major signs and symptoms are similar to those of jacksonian epilepsy, cerebral tumor, or embolus.

Diagnosis
Orange-brown eggs may be found in the feces, but a concentration procedure is necessary. Sputum specimens should be treated with 3% sodium hydroxide to dissolve the mucus and then centrifuged. Serum antibodies suggest the diagnosis, but cross-reactions with antibodies of other flukes are common. The chest x-ray film suggests pulmonary tuberculosis.

Principles of treatment
A highly effective anthelmintic agent may eliminate the need for surgery in patients with cerebral paragonimiasis.

Prevention
Health education is essential to decrease the consumption of raw foods associated with fluke infections. Raw or uncooked freshwater crabs and crayfish should not be eaten in the areas where the flukes are endemic.

Respiratory Diseases

Figure 28. The distribution of paragonimiasis.

Respiratory Diseases

Selected reading

Bia FJ, Barry M: Parasitic infections of the central nervous system. *Neurol Clin* 1986; 4:171-206.

Johnson RJ, Jong EC, Dunning SB, et al: Paragonimiasis: Diagnosis and the use of praziquantel in treatment. *Rev Infect Dis* 1985; 7:200-206.

Yokogawa M: Paragonimus and paragonimiasis. *Adv Parasitol* 1965; 3:99-158.

Q FEVER
(Query fever)

Agent
Coxiella burnetii

Distribution
Worldwide

Epidemiology
Q fever is usually an occupational disease of veterinarians, dairy workers, meat processors, or farmers who get the airborne rickettsiae from infected cattle, sheep, or wild animals. Ticks also transmit infection. Less commonly, contaminated wool, straw, fertilizer, or direct contact with materials contaminated by patients transmits the organism.

Clinical characteristics and course
After an incubation period of 2 to 3 weeks, Q fever begins abruptly with chills, fever, headache, and malaise. The most common syndrome is pneumonitis with cough and chest pain but little sputum. Endocarditis, pericarditis, and hepatitis may occur. Convalescence may be prolonged.

Diagnosis
The infectious agent for Q fever can be recovered from eggs or tissue cultures inoculated with the patient's blood or sputum. The organism is highly infectious to laboratory personnel and must be handled in appropriate containment facilities. Agglutination, fluorescent antibody, or complement fixation tests or an ELISA measures increases of antibody titers in paired sera.

Principles of treatment
Patients can be treated with antibiotics. Patients with Q fever endocarditis may require combination therapy.

Prevention
A vaccine is available for people whose occupations increase the chance of catching Q fever.

Selected reading

Baca OG, Paretsky D: Q fever and *Coxiella burnetii:* A model for host-parasite interactions. *Microbiol Rev* 1983; 47:127-149.

Ellis ME, Smith CC: Chronic or fatal Q-fever infection: A review of 16 patients seen in North-East Scotland. *Q J Med* 1983; 52:54-66.

Stephen S, Achyutha Rao KV: Q fever in India: A review. *J Indian Med Assoc* 1980; 74:200-203.

Other Diseases to Consider in the Differential Diagnosis of Respiratory Diseases in Travelers and Immigrants

BLASTOMYCOSIS
COCCIDIOIDOMYCOSIS
DIPHTHERIA
ECHINOCOCCOSIS (See page 94)
HISTOPLASMOSIS
LEGIONELLOSIS
PERTUSSIS
PSITTACOSIS
TOXOCARIASIS (See page 120)
TUBERCULOSIS
UPPER RESPIRATORY DISEASE

Gastrointestinal Diseases

AMEBIASIS

Agent
Entamoeba histolytica

Distribution
Worldwide

Epidemiology
Amebiasis is ubiquitous. Its prevalence varies from 5% in some temperate regions to 80% in some tropical regions. The trophozoite form of *E histolytica* can encyst and pass from the intestine in the feces. Humans ingest the cysts in water or food contaminated with feces.

In the intestine, the cyst wall breaks, and trophozoites are released into the lumen. The noninvasive trophozoite stays in the intestinal lumen and does not cause disease. Invasive amebic trophozoites may ingest red blood cells.

Trophozoites are rapidly destroyed by both external environmental conditions and gastric acid. However, cysts may survive in soil for at least a week at tropical temperatures and for as long as a month at lower temperatures.

Amebiasis is usually a commensal infection, and some people with commensal infections are carriers. Infected food handlers play a major role in transmitting the infection. Raw vegetables and fruit washed in contaminated water or food exposed to flies are also sources of infection.

Clinical characteristics and course
The motile trophozoite form of *E histolytica* may be invasive. The invasive trophozoite causes diarrhea and dysentery in 2% to 8% of infected people. Trophozoites that enter the bloodstream may pass to the liver or other organs and cause abscesses. Why some trophozoites invade the intestinal wall and others do not is not known. Invasiveness may be related to the strain of the parasite and its cytopathogenicity or the nutritional status and intestinal bacterial flora of the host. One or more of those factors may account for the particular pathogenicity of amebiasis in such areas as South Africa, Mexico, and India.

Amebic dysentery. The incubation period varies but is usually 2 to 4 weeks. A large proportion of patients are asymptomatic or have only a few symptoms. About three fourths of patients with invasive intestinal amebiasis note the gradual onset of colicky abdominal pain, tenesmus, and frequent stools. Patients usually pass 3 or 4 bloodstained, mucoid stools daily; but a large proportion of patients have no systemic signs. Patients with more frequent bowel movements should be examined for other concurrent causes. Diarrhea may last for weeks but commonly exacerbates and abates. In some patients, onset of dysentery is acute with fever, profuse diarrhea, dehydration, and electrolyte changes. Complications are infrequent. Possible complications of intestinal amebiasis are perforation and peritonitis, hemorrhage, strictures, and ameboma (a mass consisting of inflamed, thickened intestinal wall most commonly in the ileocecal region and in some patients mimicking malignancy).

Hepatic amebiasis. Hepatic amebiasis is characterized by abscess formation, and almost 90% of patients have single abscesses in the right lobe. Classically, patients may note sudden or gradual onset of pain in the right hypochondrium and associated fever. The liver enlarges and is tender. In a large proportion of patients, percussion sounds are decreased, and ventilation of the right lung is decreased because the diaphragm is elevated and immobile. Liver abscesses may rupture into the peritoneum or thorax or through the skin. Only a fraction of patients with amebic abscesses have intestinal infections.

Diagnosis
Symptoms of moderate diarrhea with tenesmus or dysentery in patients who have traveled in the tropics, particularly Mexico, South Africa, or India, suggest amebiasis. A definitive diagnosis can be made by finding *E histolytica* cysts or trophozoites in stool specimens or bowel wall scrapings, but that generally requires experienced microscopists. Fresh fecal samples that must be shipped to a laboratory must be preserved in polyvinyl alcohol. The best method for finding motile trophozoites containing red blood cells is microscopic examination of a wet-mounted fecal smear within one-half hour after it was voided. Rectal mucosal scrapings collected through a sigmoidoscope can also be examined. The trichrome stain defines the characteristic morphologic features of both trophozoites and cysts.

Serologic tests such as the indirect hemagglutination test may help to diagnose acute amebic dysentery because nearly all patients with the disease will have high antibody titers. Serologic test results are positive in almost all patients with amebic liver abscesses. In some cases, aspiration of a

Gastrointestinal Diseases

cyst may be necessary; and if it is, amebas may be found in the material aspirated from the abscess margin. Liver function test results are normal in a large proportion of patients with hepatic amebiasis. A liver scan will usually show the size and location of the abscess.

Principles of treatment
Amebicides and antiprotozoal agents in combination or in sequence are used to treat amebic dysentery and extraintestinal amebiasis. Asymptomatic carriers can also be treated. At least two of the drugs used are available from the Parasitic Disease Drug Service at the Centers for Disease Control in Atlanta. Large amebic abscesses in danger of rupture may require surgical drainage before specific therapy is given.

Prevention
Good hygiene is essential in the prevention of amebiasis. Handwashing by food handlers and before eating is fundamental. Where feasible, food handlers should be tested routinely, and amebiasis carriers should be excluded from food processing occupations. Fruits and vegetables should be cooked properly. Public water supplies should be protected from fecal contamination with E histolytica. Small quantities of water can be sterilized by adding 8 drops of 2% tincture of iodine per quart or by boiling. Cysts are destroyed by 5% to 10% acetic acid, 200 parts per million of iodine, or boiling; but they are not affected by the usual concentrations of chlorine used in water purification.

Selected reading

Adams EB, MacLeod IN: Invasive amebiasis. I. Amebic dysentery and its complications, and II. Amebic liver abscess and its complications. *Medicine* 1977;56:315-323, 325-334.

Gitler C, Calef E, Rosenberg I: Cytopathogenicity of *Entamoeba histolytica. Philos Trans R Soc Biol* 1984;307:73-85.

Martinez-Palomo A: *The Biology of* Entamoeba histolytica. *(Tropical Medicine Research Studies)*. New York, Research Studies Press, Inc, Division of John Wiley & Sons, Ltd, 1982.

Walsh JA: Problems in recognition and diagnosis of amebiasis: Estimation of the global magnitude of morbidity and mortality. *Rev Infect Dis* 1986; 8:228-238.

ANISAKIASIS

Agents
Larval nematodes of the family Anisakidae and the genera *Anisakis, Phocanema, Contracaecum,* and *Terranova*

Distribution
See Figure 29.

Epidemiology
Anisakidae larvae live in the gastrointestinal tracts of various edible fish. If the fish are not adequately refrigerated before they are eaten, the larvae may migrate into the fishes' muscles. If the fish are not cooked or are cooked inadequately before humans eat them, larvae liberated by stomach enzymes may penetrate the humans' gastric or intestinal mucosa. Anisakidae larvae are common in sushi and sashimi in Japan, in herring in the Netherlands and Scandinavia, and in ceviche along the Pacific coast of Latin America.

Clinical characteristics and course
A few hours after ingestion of uncooked or partially cooked fish, the gastric symptoms of anisakiasis may develop. By burrowing into the stomach wall, the larvae produce ulcers and nausea, vomiting, and abdominal pain, and in some patients, hematemesis. The larvae may migrate up the esophagus, attach to the oropharynx, and cause coughing. In the wall of the small intestine and the gastric mucosa, larvae can produce eosinophilic abscesses or granulomas with symptoms like those of appendicitis or regional enteritis. The larvae sometimes penetrate the peritoneal cavity.

Diagnosis
Gastroscopy may show the 2-cm-long larva in the oropharynx or stomach.

Principles of treatment
The larvae are removed through a gastroscope or surgically.

Prevention
Cleaning or eviscerating fish soon after they are caught and prompt refrigeration will reduce larval penetration of muscles. Fish should also be cooked adequately before being eaten. Government inspection of fish before marketing at retail outlets is important.

Gastrointestinal Diseases

Figure 29. The distribution of anisakiasis.

Gastrointestinal Diseases

Selected reading

Desowitz RS, Raybourne RB, Ishikura H, et al: The radioallergosorbent test (RAST) for the serological diagnosis of human anisakiasis. *Trans R Soc Trop Med Hyg* 1985;79:256-259.

Fontaine RE: Anisakiasis from the American perspective, editorial. *JAMA* 1985;253:1024-1025.

Lewis R, Shore JH: Anisakiasis in the United Kingdom, letter. *Lancet* 1985; 2:1019.

Sugimachi K, Inokuchi K, Doiwa T, et al: Acute gastric anisakiasis. Analysis of 178 cases. *JAMA* 1985;253:1012-1013.

ASCARIASIS
(Roundworm infection, ascaridiasis)

Agent
Ascaris lumbricoides

Distribution
Worldwide

Epidemiology
The large intestinal roundworm, *Ascaris lumbricoides*, infects one quarter of the world population. Most people in areas where the worms are endemic have small to moderate numbers of worms. In tropical countries, the prevalence of ascariasis may be greater than 50%, and infection occurs throughout the year. In dry countries, transmission occurs largely in the rainy season. Fruit and vegetables contaminated by human feces transmit the worm, and flies can transfer eggs to food. Reinfection following treatment is rapid. Children between the ages of 3 and 8 years tend to have more severe infections, and the proportion of them infected tends to be greater than that of other age groups.

When humans swallow fully embryonated eggs, the larvae hatch, penetrate the wall of the host's small intestine, and enter the bloodstream. When they reach the lungs, the larvae enter the alveoli, then crawl up the respiratory tract, and are swallowed. About 2 months after eggs have been ingested, a new generation of adult worms begins laying eggs.

Clinical characteristics and course
Feces contain eggs about 2 months after the host has ingested embryonated eggs. Intensity of infection determines whether or not symptomatic ascariasis occurs. A greater proportion of children than adults experiences symptoms. In countries where exposure is intense, the most common complications are malnutrition, biliary and intestinal obstruction, and seasonal pneumonitis. Migrating immature larvae cause pneumonitis in patients in whom symptoms have not yet developed, and migrating adult worms cause biliary and intestinal obstruction.

Biliary obstruction has been reported in substantial proportions of older children and adults with ascariasis. Nausea, vomiting, and fever occur in approximately 50% and epigastric colic in nearly all of those patients. Jaundice is rare because patients usually seek medical help.

Intestinal obstruction caused by a mass of worms in the lumen of the small bowel occurs in some young children with severe infections. The principal signs and symptoms of obstruction are vomiting and abdominal distention and pain.

Although *Ascaris* antigens are highly allergenic, pulmonary manifestations are rare. Migration of the larvae through the lungs may cause pneumonia.

Diagnosis
A patient who reports passing an adult worm may have ascariasis. Abdominal pain, nausea, and vomiting suggest intestinal obstruction; pain and fever suggest biliary obstruction; and cough and eosinophilia suggest pulmonary reactions. Most infected patients will have eaten raw vegetables and fruit.

A definitive diagnosis is made by finding eggs in the feces. A direct smear can be made in a drop of saline on a microscope slide; the high egg output obviates the need to concentrate the feces.

Principles of treatment
Several anthelmintics are effective treatments for intestinal infections.

Prevention
Travelers should avoid eating fresh leafy vegetables and unpeeled fresh fruits or vegetables. Vegetables and fruits should be washed or peeled or soaked in a solution of

Gastrointestinal Diseases

potassium permanganate before they are eaten. Proper disposal of feces must be provided, particularly in children's play areas.

Selected reading

Arfaa F: Selective primary health care: Strategies for control of disease in the developing world. XII. Ascariasis and trichuriasis. *Rev Infect Dis* 1984; 6:364-373.

Markell EK: Intestinal nematode infections. *Pediatr Clin North Am* 1985; 32:971-986.

Schultz MG: Ascariasis: Nutritional implications. *Rev Infect Dis* 1982; 4:815-819.

CHOLERA

Agent
Vibrio cholerae serovar 01 with classical biotypes and E1 Tor

Distribution
See Figure 30.

Epidemiology
The Ganges delta is regarded as the classical home of cholera because epidemics of thousands of cases occur annually. Since 1961, cholera has spread from Indonesia throughout most of Asia into eastern Europe and East and North Africa to the Iberian peninsula and Italy. Outbreaks have recurred in Japan and the South Pacific islands, and small outbreaks have occurred in Louisiana and Texas. The disease, caused by reappearance of the classic biotype, is endemic in Bangladesh and in other countries to which it has spread in the last 25 years.

Promiscuous disposal of human feces and vomitus contaminates water and food. Cholera vibrios can survive in water for long periods and may infect shellfish and other marine life. A large proportion of outbreaks outside Asia and Africa have been attributed to eating raw or poorly cooked seafood. Ninety-eight percent of infections are inapparent. In areas where the disease is endemic, large proportions of adults are immune. Poor nutrition, hypochlorhydria, and achlorhydria predispose patients to clinically overt infections. Some people with chronic infection of the bilary tract are carriers.

Clinical characteristics and course
Sudden, explosive, watery fecal discharge accompanied in some patients by vomiting follows an incubation period ranging from a few hours to 5 days, but usually from 2 to 3 days. Severe fluid loss leads to rapid dehydration, acidosis, and circulatory collapse. Patients with severe, untreated cholera may die within a few hours; fatality rates exceed 50%. Milder infections with self-limited diarrhea are common. Cholera enterotoxin induces the hypersecretion of isotonic electrolyte solution through the intact small-bowel mucosa.

Diagnosis
Diagnosis is established by recovering organisms from stool samples or vomit in appropriate culture media. Comma-shaped vibrios are visible in darkfield or phase microscopy and move in a characteristic pattern. Agglutination reactions using standard antisera determine serotypes. Increases in antibodies to cholera toxin can be measured in paired sera.

Principles of treatment
The cornerstone of cholera treatment is administration of fluids with appropriate electrolytes. Most episodes of cholera can be managed with oral solutions containing glucose (20 g/L) or sucrose (40 g/L), sodium chloride (3.5 g/L), sodium bicarbonate (2.5 g/L), and potassium choride (1.5 g/L) (see below). The volume of fluid should match fluid loss or equal 5% to 7% of body weight. Patients in shock should

Oral rehydration salt solutions	
Bicarbonate solution	
Dissolve in 1 liter of potable water:	**grams**
Sodium chloride	3.5
Sodium bicarbonate (Sodium hydrogen carbonate)	2.5
Potassium chloride	1.5
Glucose, anhydrous	20.0
Citrate solution	
Dissolve in 1 liter of potable water:	**grams**
Sodium chloride	3.5
Trisodium citrate, dihydrate	2.9
Potassium chloride	1.5
Glucose, anhydrous	20.0

Gastrointestinal Diseases

Figure 30. The distribution of cholera outbreaks since 1960.

Gastrointestinal Diseases

receive intravenous fluids containing 4 g NaCl, 1 g KCl, 6.5 g sodium acetate or 5.4 g sodium lactate, and 8 g glucose per liter or Ringer's lactate and given as rapidly as possible. Antibiotics shorten the duration of diarrhea and vibrio excretion.

Prevention

Appropriate disposal of fecal waste, handwashing, and isolation of patients are helpful. In cholera outbreaks, chemoprophylaxis with antibiotics helps to prevent infections and the spread of organisms. Where cholera is endemic, consumption of raw or uncooked seafood is unwise. Vaccines protect for 3 to 6 months about half the patients vaccinated. Ordinarily the vaccines are not recommended.

Selected reading

Feachem RG: Environmental aspects of cholera epidemiology. I. A review of selected reports of endemic and epidemic situations during 1961-1980. *Trop Dis Bull* 1981;78:675-698.

Finkelstein RA, Dorner F: Cholera enterotoxin (choleragen). *Pharmacol Ther* 1985; 27:37-47.

Hoffman SL, Moechtar MA, Simanjuntak CH, et al: Rehydration and maintenance therapy of cholera patients in Jakarta: Citrate-based versus bicarbonate-based oral rehydration salt solution. *J Infect Dis* 1985;152:1159-1165.

Miller CJ, Feachem RG, Drasar BS: Cholera epidemiology in developed and developing countries: New thoughts on transmission, seasonality, and control. *Lancet* 1985;1:261-262.

Morris JG Jr, Black RE: Cholera and other vibrioses in the United States. *N Engl J Med* 1985;312:343-350.

Steffen R: Epidemiologic studies of travelers' diarrhea, severe gastrointestinal infection, and cholera. *Rev Infect Dis* 1986;8(suppl 2):S122-S130.

CRYPTOSPORIDIOSIS

Agents
Cryptosporidium species

Distribution
Worldwide

Epidemiology
Cryptosporidium species are coccidian protozoans. From the onset of symptoms until several weeks after symptoms abate, the oocysts, the infectious stage in the life cycle, can be found in the stool. Transmission is fecal-oral, and contaminated food and liquids are possible sources of infections.

The organism is responsible for sporadic cases of diarrhea in travelers, children in day-care nurseries, and other immunocompetent people. In some studies, cryptosporidiosis has caused 2% to 4% of cases of sporadic diarrhea reported. The disease occurs more frequently and with greater severity in patients with impaired immunity than in immunocompetent patients. The impaired immunity may be caused by immunoglobulin deficiencies, AIDS, or immunosuppressive therapy; cryptosporidiosis is a particularly common complication in patients with AIDS. Animal handlers are at unusual risk.

Clinical characteristics and course
Nonbloody, watery or mucoid diarrhea begins 1 or 2 weeks after exposure and lasts 3 to 14 days. Patients may also have low-grade fever, vomiting, anorexia, abdominal cramps and pain, and weight loss. In most immunocompetent patients, the disease is self-limited to about 10 to 14 days.

Diagnosis
Experienced microbiologists can detect oocysts in fecal smears stained with Giemsa stain. The oocysts can be concentrated by sugar flotation. Modified Kinyoun acid-fast stain of a stool sample has been described as the accepted method of detection. Mucosal biopsy is not necessary in most cases.

Principles of treatment
Fluid and electrolyte imbalances should be corrected. Although no treatment has been proved effective, an antibiotic may be effective in some patients with severe or protracted infections.

Prevention
The usual rules for infections spread by feces apply; but in practice, prevention, particularly in immunocompromised patients, is impossible.

Selected reading

Casemore DP, Armstrong M, Sands RL: Laboratory diagnosis of cryptosporidiosis. *J Clin Pathol* 1985;38:1337-1341.

Gastrointestinal Diseases

Casemore DP, Sands RL, Curry A: Cryptosporidium species, a "new" human pathogen. *J Clin Pathol* 1985;38:1321-1336.

DuPont HL: Cryptosporidiosis and the healthy host. *N Engl J Med* 1985; 312:1319-1320.

Jokipii L, Pohjola S, Jokipii AM: Cryptosporidiosis associated with traveling and giardiasis. *Gastroenterology* 1985;89:838-842.

Rolston KV, Fainstein V: Cryptosporidiosis. *Eur J Clin Microbiol* 1986; 5:135-137.

Wolfson JS, Richter JM, Waldron MA, et al: Cryptosporidiosis in immunocompetent patients. *N Engl J Med* 1985;312:1278-1282.

DIARRHEA, TRAVELERS'
(See also pages 14 and 15.)

Distribution
Worldwide

Agents
Escherichia coli, Campylobacter jejuni, Campylobacter coli, or other enterotoxigenic strains that produce heat-labile or heat-stable toxins. See also amebiasis (page 86), cholera (page 90), cryptosporidiosis (page 92), food poisoning (page 98), giardiasis (page 101), salmonellosis (page 106), shigellosis (page 107), and viral gastroenteritis (page 100). Although travelers acquire viruses, they do not appear to cause diarrhea in most patients.

Epidemiology
The infectious agents that cause most travelers' diarrhea are transmitted from one person to another by food or water or both contaminated with infected feces; by utensils; or from one to another person's hands. Pathogenic *Campylobacter* organisms are found in a wide variety of rodents, birds, and domestic animals that may transmit the organisms to humans.

Intestinal flora change dramatically when people from industrialized countries visit developing countries. The chief determinant of risk is the traveler's destination; high-risk destinations include most developing countries in Latin America, Africa, the Middle East, and Asia; and moderate-risk destinations include most of southern Europe and a few Caribbean islands.

Clinical characteristics and course
The incubation period of *E coli* diarrhea is 12 to 72 hours, and the incubation periods for *C jejuni* and *C coli* vary between 3 and 5 days. Four or five loose or watery stools daily may be associated with nausea and vomiting, abdominal cramps, bloating, urgency, malaise, fever, and bloody stools in 2% to 15% of patients. Travelers' diarrhea is usually self-limited to about 3 or 4 days but may recur during a single trip. Except in infants, travelers' diarrhea is rarely life-threatening. A chronic, relapsing illness may occur with *Campylobacter* infections in as many as 20% of patients.

Diagnosis
Determination of the specific cause of the diarrhea is made by isolating the etiologic agent from stools but some experts question the need to identify the organism unless the identification will influence the patient's management.

Principles of treatment
Patients with travelers' diarrhea want relief from abdominal cramps and diarrhea. Such nonspecific agents as charcoal, bismuth, and *Lactobacillus* preparations have been used, as have antimotility and antimicrobial agents. Patients with simple diarrhea can usually balance fluids and electrolytes by ingesting potable fruit juices, soft drinks without caffeine, and salted crackers.

Patients with severe dehydration need oral rehydration with solutions of water, dextrose, NaCl and KCl, and NaHCO3 (see page 90). Patients with shock or intractable diarrhea need intravenous fluids containing sodium and potassium chloride, sodium lactate, and glucose (see page 90). Because *E coli* toxins block the resorption of water from the intestine for a short time, intensive fluid replacement is usually required for only a day or two. For severe entero-pathogenic infantile diarrhea, nonabsorbable antibiotics may be administered in divided doses for 5 days. For the rare case of severe diarrhea caused by enteroinvasive strains, oral absorbable or parenteral antibiotics should be given. For *Campylobacter* diarrhea, antibiotics are not usually required except for severe or prolonged illness.

Prevention
To prevent acute diarrhea, travelers should wash their hands before eating and eliminate fresh, unpeeled vegetables or fruit, raw meat, and raw seafood from their diets.

Gastrointestinal Diseases

When visiting countries where the risk of diarrhea is high, travelers should drink only bottled water and other bottled beverages and hot coffee or tea and avoid ice (the water source may be contaminated) and unpasteurized milk and dairy products. Many sensible precautions, even if scrupulously followed, are likely to fail because in some countries toilet and handwashing habits are so poor that prepared food becomes contaminated.

To prevent *Campylobacter* infections, all food derived from animal sources, particularly poultry, must be thoroughly cooked; milk must be pasteurized; and water must be chlorinated.

A bismuth compound and some antimicrobial agents have proved valuable as prophylaxis.

Selected reading

Consensus Conference. Travelers' diarrhea. *JAMA* 1985;253:2700-2704.

DuPont HL: Nonfluid therapy and selected chemoprophylaxis of acute diarrhea. *Am J Med* 1985;78(suppl 6B):81-90.

Edelman R: Prevention and treatment of infectious diarrhea. Speculations on the next 10 years. *Am J Med* 1985;78(suppl 6B):99-106.

Gorbach S, Edelman R (eds): Travelers' diarrhea: National Institutes of Health Consensus Development Conference. Bethesda, Maryland, January 28-30, 1985. *Rev Infect Dis* 1986;8(suppl 2):S109-S233. (14 papers)

Guerrant RL, Shields DS, Thorson SM, et al: Evaluation and diagnosis of acute infectious diarrhea. *Am J Med* 1985;78(suppl 6B):91-98.

ECHINOCOCCOSIS
(Hydatid disease)

Agent
Echinococcus granulosus, Echinococcus multilocularis, and *Echinococcus vogeli*

Distribution
See Figure 31.

Epidemiology
The larval stage of a dog tapeworm *Echinococcus granulosus* causes hydatid disease, or echinococcosis, in humans. The small adult tapeworm is found in the small intestines of dogs and wolves. The terminal gravid segments rupture and release up to 5,000 eggs, which are passed in the feces.

When suitable intermediate hosts such as sheep or humans ingest the eggs, the embryos hatch in the duodenum, penetrate the mucosa, and enter the liver where most of them are trapped in the portal system. Those that escape from the liver are usually trapped in the lungs, but some embryos may enter the systemic circulation and thus reach any organ. The life cycle is completed when dogs ingest organs containing cysts. Depending upon the conditions, eggs may survive on the ground only a few days or more than a year.

Echinococcus granulosus is highly endemic in the sheep- and cattle-raising regions of Australasia, South America, South Africa, the Soviet Union, the countries surrounding the Mediterranean, and several western states in the United States. Humans are infected most frequently by direct contact with feces from infected dogs but may also be infected by ingesting soil, vegetables, or water contaminated with eggs or by flies that carry eggs on their body surfaces.

Clinical characteristics and course
Most *E granulosus* infections are asymptomatic; and many are detected only from routine x-ray studies, investigation of unrelated conditions, or at autopsy. Within the organs, the embryos either are destroyed by inflammatory reactions or gradually develop into hydatid cysts. The size of the embryo gradually increases; and after many years, mature hydatid cysts, particularly those in the liver, may reach 20 cm in diameter. The slowly enlarging hydatid cyst is tolerated well until it becomes large enough to cause pain or dysfunction. Symptoms and signs are protean because almost any organ can be invaded. Because cysts in other sites such as bone or brain cause broken bones, pain, or neurologic signs, those cysts are detected much more rapidly than the cysts in the liver.

The anatomic distribution of cysts varies with geographic area; a representative distribution for Australia was liver: 63%; lungs: 25%; muscles: 5%; bone: 3%; kidney: 2%; spleen and brain: 1%; and the others in the heart, thyroid, breast, prostate, parotid gland, and pancreas. Approximately 20% of patients have more than one cyst. Cysts in the liver usually become quite large before producing abdominal discomfort or epigastric pain.

Calcified cysts may be the only evidence of infection or

Gastrointestinal Diseases

Figure 31. The distribution of echinococcosis infection.

● ● ● ● Areas where *Echinococcus granulosus* is reported to occur
● ● ● ● Areas of high endemicity

Gastrointestinal Diseases

patients may complain of hemoptysis, cough, and dyspnea. Brain cysts cause features of a slowly expanding lesion. Cysts in the kidney may cause hematuria or renal colic; hydatid disease of bone can cause spontaneous fractures. Acute symptoms such as urticaria and anaphylaxis may follow rupture of a cyst. Secondary hydatid cysts may develop after dissemination of scoleces from leaking cysts.

Diagnosis

Echinococcosis should be suspected in asymptomatic patients with cavitary lesions in the lungs or calcification in the liver and an occupational history of animal husbandry or close contact with dogs. Chest x-ray studies may reveal a round, uniform density with surrounding atelectasis or pneumonitis; calcification may occur. Roentgenographic evidence of fluid indicates rupture of a cyst into a bronchus. X-ray films of the abdomen may show calcified densities or a calcified cyst rim in the liver. Other useful diagnostic techniques include radioisotopic and ultrasonic scanning and computerized axial tomography (CAT).

The most specific serologic tests are agar gel precipitation or counterelectroimmunophoresis with a precipitin band at arc 5. The counterelectroimmunophoresis test is not readily available and has been reported to yield a large proportion of false-negative results. Other useful serologic tests are indirect hemagglutination, indirect immunofluorescence, latex agglutination, and ELISA. Diagnostic specificity of those tests varies from 60% to 90%. Antibodies in serum specimens suggest echinococcosis.

Percutaneous needle puncture of a cyst should not be attempted because this procedure may cause leakage that could cause anaphylaxis or spread of the lesions.

Principles of treatment

Surgical resection of isolated cysts is the treatment of choice. If the cyst is likely to rupture, the contents can be sterilized with an injection of hypertonic saline solution. An anthelmintic given for a long time is sometimes effective, particularly if cysts have not been broken surgically or accidentally.

Prevention

In areas of livestock production, safe disposal of infected viscera is essential. Dogs should be tested periodically for infection and treated for echinococcosis.

Selected reading

Elliot DL, Tolle SW, Goldberg L, et al: Pet-associated illness. *N Engl J Med* 1985;313:985-995.

Grabbe E, Kern P, Heller M: Human echinococcosis: Diagnostic value of computed tomography. *Tropenmed Parasitol* 1981;32:35-38.

Little JM: Hydatid disease at Royal Prince Alfred Hospital, 1964 to 1974. *Med J Aust* 1976;1:903-908.

O'Leary P: A five-year review of human hydatid cyst disease in Turkana district, Kenya. *East Afr Med J* 1976;53:540-544.

Rickard MD, Williams JF: Hydatidosis/cysticercosis: Immune mechanisms and immunization against infection. *Adv Parasitol* 1982;21:229-296.

FLUKE DISEASE

Agents

Fasciolopsis buski, Clonorchis sinensis, Opisthorchis felineus, Opisthorchis viverrini, and *Fasciola hepatica*

Distribution

See Figure 32.

Epidemiology

Flukes, or trematodes, are parasitic flatworms with unique life cycles comprising asexual reproduction in the snail intermediate host and sexual reproduction in the human definitive host. People become infected with flukes except for *F hepatica*, which is rare, only in Asia. For descriptions of *Paragonimus* species and blood flukes, see pages 83 and 69.

F buski lives in pigs and humans in the Far East, Southeast Asia, and the Indian subcontinent. The cercariae of *F buski* flukes leave the snail and encyst on certain water plants where the parasites become infective metacercariae. Humans ingest the plants, and the metacercariae mature into adult worms that produce eggs. They pass into fresh water, hatch into free-swimming miracidia that penetrate certain species of snails, and replicate.

The liver flukes, *C sinensis, O felineus,* and *O viverrini,* develop in operculate snails, which excrete cercariae that penetrate under the scales or into the flesh of about 80

Gastrointestinal Diseases

Figure 32. The distribution of fluke disease.

●●●● C sinensis
●●●● F buski
●●●● C sinensis, F buski
●●●● O viverrini, F buski

Gastrointestinal Diseases

species of freshwater fish and encyst. When humans eat raw or inadequately cooked infected fish, the organisms excyst in the duodenum; and the larvae pass directly into the bile ducts where they mature into adult worms. They produce large numbers of eggs that pass through the bile ducts into the intestines and into the water in the feces.

C sinensis, O felineus, and O viverrini are commonly found in cats and dogs but also infect many other mammals. Clonorchiasis is prevalent in China, Hong Kong, Vietnam, Korea, Japan, and Taiwan. O felineus infections have been reported in many parts of Southeast Asia as well as in Europe and the USSR, and O viverrini is prevalent in Thailand and Laos.

The cercariae of F hepatica pass out of snails and encyst on the leaves of freshwater plants such as watercress. When humans eat the plants, the larvae excyst, pass through the gut wall into the peritoneal cavity, and enter the liver through its capsule. Young flukes migrate through the tissues of the liver for 6 to 9 weeks and then penetrate the bile ducts where they mature and begin to produce eggs. The eggs pass out of the bile ducts and are excreted in the feces. In fresh water, the eggs mature and then hatch into miracidia that penetrate certain species of snails and continue to develop. The organisms cause significant mortality in sheep and cattle worldwide. Sporadic infections in humans have occurred in South America, Africa, China, and Australia and have usually been associated with ingestion of wild watercress.

Clinical characteristics and course

Most patients with fasciolopsiasis have no detectable signs or symptoms of disease. However, patients with large numbers of worms may have diarrhea; abdominal pain; and edema of the face, trunk, and legs; and pass undigested food in the feces.

Clonorchiasis and opisthorchiasis tend to be silent infections. Severe chronic infections may result in cholangitis, cholangiohepatitis, and cholangiocarcinoma.

In some patients, fascioliasis can cause acute signs and symptoms as larvae migrate within the liver. The patients suffer from prolonged fever, pain in the right hypochondrium, severe eosinophilia, and sometimes hepatomegaly. Those signs and symptoms abate and then disappear completely after the flukes enter the bile ducts. The bile ducts may become obstructed and inflammation may follow.

Diagnosis

The definitive diagnosis is made by finding fluke eggs in the feces of the patient, but that is not always possible in the early stages of some infections.

Principles of treatment

Anthelmintics usually cure liver or intestinal fluke infections.

Prevention

Health education is essential to decrease the consumption of raw foods associated with fluke infections. Where infected humans are important sources of eggs for maintenance of the clonorchiasis, opisthorchiasis, and fasciolopsiasis cycles, sanitary disposal of human feces and good personal hygiene are required. To prevent clonorchiasis, all contaminated freshwater fish must be cooked thoroughly.

Selected reading

Harinasuta T, Riganti M, Bunnag D: Opisthorchis viverrini infection: Pathogenesis and clinical features. Arzneimittelforsch 1984;34B:1167-1169.

International Symposium on Human Trematode Infections in Southeast and East Asia. Kyongju, Republic of Korea, October 19-21, 1983. Proceedings. Arzneimittelforsch 1984;34:1115-1240.

Plaut AG, Min DY: Remarks on the diagnosis of Clonorchis sinensis infection. Arzneimittelforsch 1984;34B:1153-1156.

Min HK: Clonorchis sinensis: Pathogenesis and clinical features of infection. Arzneimittelforsch 1984;34B:1151-1153.

Schwartz DA: Cholangiocarcinoma associated with liver fluke infection: A preventable source of morbidity in Asian immigrants. Am J Gastroenterol 1986;81:76-79.

Webbe G: Human trematode infections. J Trop Med Hyg 1984;87:147-151.

FOOD POISONING

Distribution

Worldwide

Agents

This section concerns illnesses caused by the ingestion

Gastrointestinal Diseases

Table 23
Microbial agents, incubation periods, sources, and symptoms of food poisoning.

Agent	Incubation periods, gastrointestinal signs	Sources, symptoms other than gastroenteritis, and distribution
Bacillus cereus	1-6 hours: nausea and vomiting; 6-16 hours: diarrhea, abdominal cramps	Rice, vegetables, and meat kept at room temperature for many hours after cooking.
Clostridium botulinum	2-36 hours: nausea, vomiting, diarrhea, paralysis	Inadequately heated canned food eaten without subsequent cooking. Common sources in the United States are vegetables and fruits and in Europe and Japan are meats and fish. Ptosis, blurred or double vision, dry mouth, and sore throat are early symptoms. Vomiting, diarrhea, and descending flaccid paralysis may follow. Respiratory failure and death may occur.
Clostridium perfringens	10-12 hours: diarrhea, abdominal cramps, and in some people, nausea	Food contaminated with soil or feces and inadequately cooked or reheated food. Outbreaks associated with caterers, restaurants, cafeterias, schools.
Gambierdisus toxicus (Ciguatera fish poisoning)	4-6 hours: nausea, vomiting, diarrhea, abdominal cramps	Consumption of moray eel, barracuda, red snapper, grey snapper, grouper, or shark that have consumed smaller fish that feed on coral reef protozoans. Symptoms include itching, prickling of lips, weakness, and muscle pain. Predominantly a problem in tropical and subtropical areas of the Pacific, Indian Ocean, and the Caribbean.
Staphylococcus aureus	2-4 hours: vomiting and perhaps diarrhea	Poorly cooked or unrefrigerated food such as pastries, custards, salad dressings, sandwiches, sliced meats.
Vibrio parahaemolyticus	12-24 hours: diarrhea, abdominal cramps	Raw or inadequately cooked seafood held at room temperature for hours, contamination of food with raw seafood or seawater. Some patients may have a fever.

of food or fluids contaminated with toxic substances such as heavy metals, organic substances that are natural components of some foods, or substances elaborated by microorganisms. The list of agents includes *Staphylococcus aureus, Clostridium botulinum, Clostridium perfringens, Vibrio parahaemolyticus, Bacillus cereus,* bacteria found in ciguatera and scombroid fish, protozoa, mushrooms, copper, cadmium, zinc, and tin. Other organisms responsible are *Campylobacter jejuni, Escherichia coli, Vibrio cholerae* (page 90), and *Salmonella* (page 106).

Epidemiology
The modes of transmission and distribution of microbial agents that cause food poisoning appear in Table 23. In addition, about 50 species of mushrooms contain toxic substances. Heavy metals can be ingested in acidic and carbonated beverages stored in or served from corroded metal containers.

Diagnosis
Generally food poisoning is recognized when the same signs and symptoms occur at the same time in several people who ate the same food. The food responsible for the poisoning may not have not been cooked or refrigerated adequately or both or may have been prepared or served by people with contaminated hands. The specific agent responsible can be determined by culturing the organism or identifying a toxin in food, serum, or stool. The heavy

Gastrointestinal Diseases

metals and chemical poisons are identified by biologic, immunologic, or chemical tests.

Principles of treatment

Fluid should be replaced if necessary in people infected with S aureus, C perfringens, V parahaemolyticus, or B cereus toxins. Patients who have ingested C botulinum should receive intravenously and intramuscularly trivalent antitoxin A, B, and E available from the Centers for Disease Control. Patients with ciguatera poisoning need supportive care. Patients with heavy metal poisoning may respond to chelating agents.

Prevention

Food that is or has been kept at room temperature for prolonged periods should not be eaten. To prevent botulism, bulging cans should not be opened and food from bulging cans or food that smells bad should not be used or tasted. No means of preparing fish will inactivate ciguatoxin, which is tasteless and odorless. However, a radioimmunoassay can detect toxin in fish before it is marketed. Large fish are especially dangerous. The viscera, especially the liver, should not be eaten.

Selected reading

Gelb AM, Mildvan D: Ciguatera fish poisoning. NY State J Med 1979; 79:1080-1081.

Grant IC: Ciguatera poisoning. J R Nav Med Service 1984;70:82-86.

Joseph SW, Colwell RR, Kaper JB: Vibrio parahaemolyticus and related halophilic vibrios. CRC Crit Rev Microbiol 1982;10:77-124.

Noah ND: ABC of nutrition. Food poisoning. Br Med J 1985;291:879-883.

Woolaway MC, Bartlett CL, Wieneke AA, et al: International outbreak of staphylococcal food poisoning caused by contaminated lasagne. J Hyg 1986;96(1):67-73.

GASTROENTERITIS, VIRAL

Agents

Rotaviruses of four serotypes cause Rotavirus enteritis primarily in infants and young children. Other agents of viral gastroenteritis are Norwalk agent and numerous viruses in the calicivirus, adenovirus, astrovirus, or coronavirus families. Except for Norwalk agent, those viruses are often associated with epidemic viral gastroenteropathy.

Distribution

Worldwide

Epidemiology

Viruses are probably spread person to person via fecal-oral or oral-oral contact or by aerosol. Rotaviruses are associated with up to 50% of the episodes of severe diarrhea in infants and children. In developing countries, viral gastroenteritis occurs continuously rather than in outbreaks or epidemics. Norwalk and other agents may cause epidemics of gastroenteritis that last 1 to 2 days in all age groups at any time of year.

Clinical characteristics and course

After an incubation period of 2 days, Rotavirus enteritis may begin with severe diarrhea and vomiting. One to two days after the patient has been exposed to the virus, epidemic viral gastroenteropathy may cause any or all of the following: nausea, vomiting, diarrhea, abdominal pain, myalgia, headache, and low-grade fever.

Diagnosis

Diagnosis is confirmed by immune electron microscopic identification of the agent in the stool or by detection of increased Rotavirus antibody by an ELISA or by complement fixation, fluorescent antibody, or neutralization tests of paired sera.

Principles of treatment

Many patients require prompt fluid replacement, preferably by the oral route. Oral salt solutions (see page 90) may be particularly effective for early treatment of diarrhea in children.

Prevention

The viral infections may be prevented by careful handwashing and good household hygiene.

Selected reading

Kapikian AZ, Wyatt RG, Greenberg HB, et al: Approaches to immunization of infants and young children against gastroenteritis due to rotaviruses. Rev Infect Dis 1980;2:459-469.

Gastrointestinal Diseases

Sack DA, Eusof A, Merson MH, et al: Oral rehydration in rotavirus diarrhea: A double blind comparison of sucrose with glucose electrolyte solution. *Lancet* 1978; 2:280-283.

Yolken RH, Miotti P, Viscidi R: Immunoassays for the diagnosis and study of viral gastroenteritis. *Pediatr Infect Dis* 1986;5:S46-S52.

GIARDIASIS
(Giardia enteritis, lambliasis)

Agent
Giardia lamblia

Distribution
Worldwide

Epidemiology
Giardia lamblia is a flagellate protozoan that causes acute and chronic diarrhea and malabsorption. The organism exists in two forms, trophozoites and cysts, which live in the upper small intestine of humans. The stools of infected patients usually contain cysts, the infective stage of the parasite. They survive in water for 3 months or longer despite the addition of chlorine; the cysts can be filtered out of drinking water. Most cysts are water-borne although some are ingested with food and some are transmitted from person to person. Ingested cysts excyst in the duodenum and divide into two trophozoites that remain there and in the upper jejunum.

G *lamblia* has been found in monkeys, pigs, dogs, and beavers. Cysts from infected beavers have infected human volunteers. Severe disease occurs in children and malnourished people of all ages. Travelers are especially likely to catch giardiasis where unfiltered surface water is used.

Clinical characteristics
Where giardiasis is endemic, most infected people have no symptoms. In other people giardial diarrhea begins between 1 and 3 weeks, usually 7 to 10 days, after infection. The stools are loose, greasy, and sometimes watery. They may contain mucus but rarely blood. Prolonged diarrhea may cause substantial weight loss, and steatorrhea and malabsorption may develop. Other symptoms are upper abdominal discomfort, bloating, and nausea. In a small proportion of patients, symptoms abate spontaneously after several days, but in most patients, symptoms wax and wane for some time. Giardiasis has been implicated in the chronic diarrhea and malabsorption often observed in patients with dysgammaglobulinemia.

Diagnosis
Giardiasis should be considered as a possible cause of persistent diarrhea, malabsorption, or weight loss, particularly in patients who have traveled to Leningrad, any tropical area, or the Rocky Mountain areas of Canada and the United States. Patients may have increased D-xylose absorption and decreased serum folate, urinary excretion of vitamin B_{12}, and fecal fat. Direct fecal smears may contain *G lamblia* trophozoites or cysts; concentration techniques will improve the sensitivity of the examination. Persistent negative stool examinations may necessitate sampling duodenal contents either by intubation and aspiration or with a string test.

Principles of treatment
Certain anthelmintic, antiprotozoal, and antibacterial agents will usually cure giardiasis. Some patients may require more than one course of therapy.

Prevention
Since ordinary chlorination does not kill *Giardia* cysts, public water supplies must be filtered through sand, particularly where zoonotic sources of *Giardia* contamination are common. Small supplies of drinking water can be made safe by boiling or treatment with 0.5 mL of 2% tincture of iodine per liter held for 20 minutes or longer if the water is cold.

Selected reading

Brodsky RE, Spencer HC Jr, Schultz MG: Giardiasis in American travelers to the Soviet Union. *J Infect Dis* 1974; 130:319-323.

Dupont HL, Sullivan PS: Giardiasis: The clinical spectrum, diagnosis, and therapy. *Pediatr Infect Dis* 1986; 5:S131-S138.

Gillon J: Giardiasis: Review of epidemiology, pathogenetic mechanisms and host responses. *Q J Med* 1984;53:23-39.

Jokipii AMM, Hemila M, Jokipii L: Prospective study of acquisition of cryptosporidium, *Giardia lamblia*, and gastrointestinal illness. *Lancet* 1985; 1:487-489.

Smith PD: Pathophysiology and immunology of giardiasis. *Annu Rev Med* 1985; 36:295-307.

Gastrointestinal Diseases

HEPATITIS, VIRAL
(For other names, see Table 24.)

Agents
Hepatitis A virus (HAV), heptatitis B virus (HBV), delta hepatitis virus (possibly an incomplete RNA virus), epidemic non-A, non-B hepatitis virus or viruses, posttransfusion non-A, non-B hepatitis virus or viruses.

Distribution
Worldwide

Epidemiology
See Table 24.

Clinical characteristics and course
HAV infection. Malaise, anorexia, nausea, abdominal discomfort, and fever appear abruptly and are followed in a few days by light-colored stools, dark urine, and jaundice. HAV infection usually lasts 1 to 2 weeks, and cure is complete. Few patients die.

HBV infection. Onset is insidious with the same signs and symptoms as HAV infection, and severity varies widely. In certain populations, particularly in infants, persistent antigenemia and chronic hepatitis are common sequelae.

Delta hepatitis. Onset is abrupt and in a large proportion of patients severe. All patients have coexisting HBV infection or carry the hepatitis B surface antigen (HBsAg).

Epidemic non-A, non-B hepatitis. The characteristics of epidemic hepatitis are the same as those of HAV infection.

Posttransfusion non-A, non-B hepatitis. Onset is insidious with the same symptoms and signs as epidemic non-A, non-B hepatitis. Severity varies widely. In certain populations, particularly in infants, persistent antigenemia and chronic hepatitis are common sequelae.

Diagnosis
HAV infection. The screening test measures increased titers of HAV-specific IgG antibodies although IgM antibodies are produced. Both can be measured by an ELISA or a radioimmunoassay of paired sera or acute phase serum. Increased IgG titers indicate that the infection is acute or recent.

HBV infection. This causes production of HBsAg, core antigen (HBcAg), or e antigen (HBeAg) and then the corresponding antibodies. Chronic active hepatitis causes production of circulating HBe. Anti-HBc IgM can usually be detected for up to 6 months after acute illness ends.

Delta hepatitis. This causes production of IgM antibody or seroconversion to delta antigen, which can be measured in paired sera with a radioimmunoassay or an ELISA.

Epidemic non-A, non-B hepatitis. This can be diagnosed only by excluding HAV and HBV and the possibility that the hepatitis was transmitted parenterally. No serologic test is available.

Posttransfusion non-A, non-B hepatitis. This can be diagnosed by excluding HAV and HBV hepatitis with appropriate tests of paired sera for seroconversion to HAV antigen or circulating HBsAg.

Principles of treatment
Hepatitis patients need supportive care and bed rest.

Prevention
HAV infection. Pooled human gamma globulin (IgG) prophylaxis is valuable for most travelers. Appropriate doses of IgG prevent hepatitis for up to 6 months. IgG prepared in the United States does not cause HBV infection or AIDS.

HBV infection. Hepatitis B immune globulin and vaccines prepared from antigenemic human plasma or products of genetic engineering are useful for people in high-risk occupations or known to have been exposed. Blood bank products are screened to eliminate HBV antigen. Opportunities for parenteral transmission by means such as sharing needles among drug users or close-contact transmission must be reduced.

Delta hepatitis. No effective preventive measures exist.

Epidemic non-A, non-B hepatitis. Good personal hygiene may reduce the risk of transmission as it does for other agents transferred from human feces to hands, food, or water.

Posttransfusion non-A, non-B hepatitis. Opportunities for close-contact transmission must be reduced. No effective preventative measures exist.

Selected reading

Anderson BN, Coulepis AG, Gust ID: Towards a hepatitis A vaccine. A review. *J Hyg* 1984;93:269-276.

Bredfeldt JE: Hepatitis B virus. Update on the spectrum of clinical infection and on prophylaxis. *Postgrad Med* 1985;78:71-78, 81-83.

Gastrointestinal Diseases

Table 24
Causes, common names, incubation periods, and modes of transmission of hepatitis.

Agent	Incubation period	Modes of transmission
Hepatitis A virus (Infectious hepatitis, epidemic hepatitis, or jaundice)	15-50 days	Person to person, fecal-oral route. Contaminated food, milk, water, uncooked mollusks.
Hepatitis B virus (Serum hepatitis, homologous serum hepatitis)	45-180 days	Percutaneous inoculation of virus, particularly in people with circulating hepatitis B antigen. This mode of transmission includes transfusion of blood and blood products, use of contaminated needles, sexual intercourse, contamination of abrasions or lacerations with infective blood, and perinatal transmission by infected mothers of susceptible infants. At high risk are homosexuals, hemophiliacs, and health care workers.
Delta hepatitis virus	Possibly 2-10 weeks	Thought to be similar to transmission of hepatitis B virus.
Epidemic non-A, non-B hepatitis virus (Fecal-oral non-A, non-B hepatitis)	15-64 days	Thought to be similar to transmission of hepatitis A virus.
Posttransfusion non-A, non-B hepatitis virus (Hepatitis C)	Usually 6-9 weeks (Range: 2 weeks to 9 months)	Similar to transmission of hepatitis B virus.

Deinhardt F: The agents of human viral hepatitis, and control of the disease. *Prog Med Virol* 1984;30:14-28.

Leads from the MMWR. Recommendations for protection against viral hepatitis. *JAMA* 1985;254:29-30, 35-36, 197-198, 203-205, 210-211, 217.

Shorey J: The current status of non-A, non-B viral hepatitis. *Am J Med Sci* 1985;289:251-261.

Wick MR, Moore S, Taswell HF: Non-A, non-B hepatitis associated with blood transfusion. *Transfusion* 1985;25:93-101.

HOOKWORM
(Ancylostomiasis, uncinariasis)

Agents
Ancylostoma duodenale and *Necator americanus* hookworms

Distribution
See Figure 33.

Epidemiology
Two major species of hookworms infect humans. When hookworm eggs in feces are deposited onto suitable soil, they hatch and molt twice; and the larvae become infective in humans. The larvae penetrate human skin in contact with contaminated soil for as little as 5 to 10 minutes. Larvae eventually attach to the wall of the small intestine, where they produce eggs and ingest blood and mucosal substances, much of which they excrete. The average blood loss from *N americanus* infection is 0.03 mL of blood per worm per day, but blood loss is about ten times higher, 0.26 mL of blood per worm per day, in patients with *A duodenale* infections. In patients with severe infections, blood loss may be severe enough to cause iron deficiency anemia.

Hookworm infections are particularly common in the agrarian areas of tropical Africa, Asia, Central and South America, and the Caribbean. Both species are found in most of those regions. The parasites thrive where the soil is

Gastrointestinal Diseases

Figure 33. The distribution of human hookworm infection.

Gastrointestinal Diseases

Figure 34. Cutaneous larva migrans.

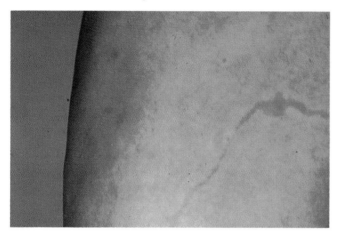

moderately moist, shaded, and well aerated and where temperatures range between 23° and 33° C.

Clinical characteristics and course

While hundreds of millions of people have hookworm infections, only a small fraction with large numbers of worms have hookworm disease.

Depending upon the intensity of infection, symptoms appear within weeks to months after exposure. After the first exposure to larvae, the skin reaction is very mild, but repeated exposures may cause *ground itch,* a syndrome that includes pruritus, edema, erythema, and papulovesicular rash. Usually as the larvae pass through the lung, few symptoms occur; but severe experimental infections have caused coughing and wheezing. A small proportion of patients with severe infections complain of epigastric discomfort and tenderness. Dog and cat hookworms can migrate intracutaneously and cause creeping eruptions (Figure 34), particularly in children.

Patients with chronic severe infections have few symptoms until anemia becomes moderate or severe. Then patients may complain of fatigue, headache, numbness, tingling, dyspnea, palpitations, anorexia, dyspepsia, swollen ankles, and sexual dysfunction. Children may fail to grow, become irritable, and have behavior problems and impaired intellectual function. Physical findings include dependent edema that may be due in part to protein loss, pallor, tachycardia, dyspnea, and palpitations. The only consistent laboratory findings are anemia and iron deficiency and hypoalbuminemia in patients with severe infections.

Diagnosis

Hookworm should be suspected in patients with symptoms of iron deficiency anemia and a history of travel in rural tropical or semitropical areas. If the patient also has hypoalbuminemia and documented anemia, the likelihood of hookworm infection increases. Finding eggs in the feces establishes the diagnosis. The eggs of N americanus and A duodenale are indistinguishable. For epidemiologic studies, the species of the hookworm can be determined by examining adult worms expelled after treatment or larvae after they have been cultured from eggs.

Direct fecal smears are screened for hookworm eggs. This technique identifies eggs when counts exceed 1,000/mL, a concentration well below those associated with anemia. High egg counts suggest that anemia is due to hookworm disease, but other common sources of anemia should be sought. If necessary, quantitative techniques, in particular the modified Stoll method, can be used.

Principles of treatment

Single doses of certain anthelmintics are effective and cause few if any side effects. Red blood cell count will increase slowly in treated patients without supplemental dietary iron, but progress will be slow. Stools should be examined 2 weeks after the anthelmintic is given and therapy repeated if a heavy hookworm burden persists.

Prevention

To prevent hookworm, feces must be safely disposed of, and people in the tropics must wear shoes or sandals. Prolonged exposure of any area of skin to soil contaminated with infective larvae can produce an infection.

Selected reading

Gilman RH: Hookworm disease: Host-pathogen biology. *Rev Infect Dis* 1982; 4:824-829.

Markell EK: Intestinal nematode infections. *Pediatr Clin North Am* 1985; 32:971-986.

Miller TA: Hookworm infection in man. *Adv Parasitol* 1979;17:315-384.

Roche M, Layrisse M: The nature and causes of "hookworm anemia." *Am J Trop Med Hyg* 1955;15:1030-1100.

Gastrointestinal Diseases

Schad GA, Banwell JG: Hookworms, in Warren KS, Mahmoud AAF (eds): *Tropical and Geographical Medicine*. New York, McGraw-Hill Book Co, 1984, pp 359-372.

Variyam EP, Banwell JG: Hookworm disease: Nutritional implications. *Rev Infect Dis* 1982;4:830-835.

SALMONELLOSIS

Agents
Salmonella serotypes

Distribution
Worldwide

Epidemiology
Two thousand serotypes of *Salmonella* can cause enterocolitis (gastroenteritis) in a large number of animals and in humans. Salmonellosis often occurs in small outbreaks, mostly in young children; larger outbreaks occur in institutions. Cases that appear to be isolated usually are not; other people associated with the patient have unrecognized infections. Restaurant-associated disease is particularly common in developing countries. Important sources of infection include raw eggs, unpasteurized milk, poultry, meat, and unsterilized animal products such as sausages or meat pies. *Salmonella* bacilli grow in food at room temperature. Meat or poultry products processed with contaminated utensils or on contaminated work surfaces are important sources of infection. The infection can also be water-borne or transmitted from human to human. Organisms are readily spread by the fecal-oral route from infected people with or without symptoms. Bacteria may be excreted in stools for days to weeks following acute illness.

Clinical characteristics and course
An incubation period of 6 to 72 hours, but usually 12 to 36 hours, precedes sudden onset of headache, abdominal pain, diarrhea that may persist for several days, fever, nausea, and in some patients vomiting. *Salmonella* organisms occasionally cause septicemia accompanied by fever, chills, sweats, malaise, anorexia, and weight loss and produce local infections such as cholecystitis, endocarditis, pericarditis, pneumonia, pyelonephritis, arthritis, meningitis, or pyoderma.

Dehydration may cause rapid death in young infants.

Diagnosis
Salmonella organisms can be isolated from feces of patients with diarrhea or from the blood of patients with septicemia. Moderate numbers of polymorphonuclear leukocytes can be found in stool samples.

Principles of treatment
Patients with uncomplicated *Salmonella* infections need no treatment other than oral rehydration. Antibiotics are recommended for infants under 2 months of age, elderly or debilitated patients, or patients with extraintestinal infections. Some *Salmonella* strains have become resistant to certain antibiotics.

Prevention
Cooked or uncooked food held at ambient temperature is the most likely source of infection. Because inadequately cooked egg products or inadequately pasteurized milk products are hazardous, ice cream may be unsafe.

Toilet customs in many developing countries involve use of hands rather than toilet paper, and soap is rarely provided for handwashing. People recovering from *Salmonella* infections or carrying the organisms and employed as food handlers or waiters may contaminate food, water, or eating utensils. In such countries eating only hot food and drinking only hot or bottled beverages may be the best preventative. In most studies of travelers' diarrhea, *Salmonella* infection rates are related to the length of stay and to residence in homes instead of hotels.

Selected reading

Buchwald DS, Blaser MJ: A review of human salmonellosis: II. Duration of excretion following infection with non-typhi Salmonella. *Rev Infect Dis* 1984; 6:345-356.

Cherubin CE: Antibiotic resistance of *Salmonella* in Europe and the United States. *Rev Infect Dis* 1981;3:1105-1126.

Smith SM, Palumbo PE, Edelson PJ: *Salmonella* strains resistant to multiple antibiotics: Therapeutic implications. *Pediatr Infect Dis* 1984;3:455-460.

Stephen J, Wallis TS, Starkey WG, et al: Salmonellosis: In retrospect and prospect. *CIBA Found Symp* 1985;112:175-192.

Gastrointestinal Diseases

SHIGELLOSIS
(Bacillary dysentery)

Agents
Four subgenera of *Shigella* bacilli are pathogenic in humans. Virulence is associated with a specific plasmid.

Distribution
Worldwide

Epidemiology
Shigellosis is endemic in tropical and temperate climates, but crowding and poor sanitation make infection a particular hazard in developing countries. Nonetheless, in the US in 1980 over 14,000 cases were reported. Commonly, people who have had recent infections or carriers whose hands are contaminated with fecal material contaminate food, fluids, utensils, and tableware. Since 10 to 100 organisms can initiate infection, hand-to-hand contact may transmit the disease. After symptomatic infections, untreated people may excrete organisms in feces for up to 4 weeks or longer. The disease is most severe in children and the elderly or debilitated.

Clinical characteristics and course
After an incubation period of 1 to 7 days, usually 24 to 72 hours, shigellosis causes acute, watery diarrhea and intense abdominal pain; and vomiting; and in some patients high fever and myalgia. In the second stage, shigellosis causes dysentery with reduced diarrhea with red blood and mucus and tenesmus. Usually self-limited, shigellosis lasts 4 to 7 days. *Shigella dysenteriae* often causes severe disease with a fatality rate as high as 20% among hospitalized patients.

Diagnosis
Suspect shigellosis when the stools of patients with classical symptoms contain large numbers of polymorphonuclear cells. Organisms can be isolated from feces or rectal swabs.

Principles of treatment
Fluid and electrolyte replacement are essential; and in a large proportion of patients, oral rehydration salt solutions can be used (see page 90). Certain antibiotics shorten the course of severe illness and the duration of excretion of organisms. The antibiotic selected must match the susceptibility pattern of the infectious organism.

Prevention
The same principles outlined for salmonellosis should be followed (see page 106). Wastes should be disposed of carefully, and the water supply should be made safe. All patients and contacts should wash their hands thoroughly, particularly when caring for young children. Infection can be caused by very small numbers of organisms.

Selected reading

Keusch GT, Donohue-Rolfe A, Jacewicz M: Shigella toxin(s): Description and role in diarrhea and dysentery. *Pharmacol Ther* 1981;15:403-438.

Shigellosis among tourists – Union of Soviet Socialist Republics, 1983. *MMWR* 1984;33:234-235.

STRONGYLOIDIASIS

Agent
Strongyloides stercoralis

Distribution
Worldwide

Epidemiology
The prevalence of strongyloidiasis is less than that of other nematode infections, but distribution is wide in the tropics and uneven in temperate regions. Most imported infections are found in immigrants from the Caribbean and in military personnel stationed in the tropics. *S stercoralis* is unique among helminths because it can cause internal or external autoinfection. *S stercoralis* may have three different life cycles: free-living, parasitic, and autoinfectious.

In the *free-living cycle*, rhabditiform larvae passed in the feces molt and differentiate into free-living males and females. Their numerous fertilized eggs hatch into free-living, rhabditiform larvae. They may develop into free-living adults and continue the cycle or change into filariform larvae that infect humans.

In the *parasitic cycle*, filariform larvae penetrate the skin of humans, and fertilized females eventually penetrate the mucosal epithelium of the upper small intestine. The eggs they deposit hatch rapidly within the intestinal wall and enter the lumen, and first-stage rhabditiform larvae are

Gastrointestinal Diseases

passed in the feces. Those larvae develop in a day or two into infective filariform larvae.

In the *autoinfectious cycle,* development is accelerated; and the rhabditiform larvae change into infective filariform larvae in the lumen of the intestine. The infective larvae penetrate the intestinal mucosa or the perianal skin after being passed in the stool and migrate through the lungs to the small intestine to reinfect the host. Occasionally, the rhabditiform larvae transform into filariform larvae in the intestinal mucosa. These cycles perpetuate the infection for many years and can produce overwhelming disease.

Clinical characteristics and course
About 2 weeks elapse between penetration of the skin by filariform larvae and the appearance of rhabditiform larvae in the feces. Some people with S *stercoralis* infections are asymptomatic or have only vague abdominal symptoms. The onset of symptoms varies.

Repeated acute infection may cause urticarial, pruritic, papular, or erythematous rashes. In some patients, coughing, shortness of breath, wheezing, and fever may occur as the larvae migrate through the lungs. If the fertilized female worms invade the intestinal mucosa, intestinal signs and symptoms, such as epigastric burning and abdominal pain possibly exacerbated by eating, may occur. Diarrhea with mucus is common and in some patients alternates with constipation. Periodic attacks of diarrhea may occur for many years and cause weight loss.

Patients with autoinfections may have larva currens, serpiginous wheals caused by migration of larva from the perianal region to the buttocks, abdomen, and thighs. Severe autoinfection, which occurs in some immunosuppressed patients, may evolve into massive systemic strongyloidiasis with general abdominal pain, distention, and shock. Patients may have high fevers and gram-negative septicemia that causes pneumonia or meningitis. Eosinophilia, common in patients with milder infections, usually does not occur in patients with systemic autoinfection.

Diagnosis
Strongyloidiasis should be suspected in patients with urticaria, abdominal pain, diarrhea, or eosinophilia. Larvae in fecal smears provide a definitive diagnosis, but usually the feces must be concentrated first with one of the standard methods, such as formalin-ether sedimentation. If several fecal samples are negative, duodenal contents may have to be sampled through a tube or with the string test. The sputum of patients with hyperinfection may contain larvae.

Principles of treatment
Because autoinfection may occur, all infected patients should be treated with an anthelmintic. Hyperinfections must be diagnosed as rapidly as possible, and vigorous treatment must be instituted early. Drug therapy is not always effective, and patients should be reevaluated after initial treatment.

Prevention
Strongyloidiasis can best be prevented by sanitary disposal of fecal waste and by wearing shoes.

Selected reading

Grove DI: Strongyloidiasis in Allied ex-prisoners of war in Southeast Asia. *Br Med J* 1980;1:598-601.

Igra-Siegman Y, Kapila R, Sen P, et al: Syndrome of hyperinfection with *Strongyloides stercoralis. Rev Infect Dis* 1981;3:397-407.

Neva F: Biology and immunology of human strongyloidiasis. *J Infect Dis* 1986;153:397-406.

Markell EK: Intestinal nematode infections. *Pediatr Clin North Am* 1985; 32:971-976.

TAPEWORM INFECTIONS AND CYSTICERCOSIS

Agents
Taenia saginata, Taenia solium, Diphyllobothrium latum, and *Hymenolepis nana*

Distribution
Worldwide

Epidemiology
The length of tapeworms ranges from microscopic to 10 to 30 feet. Ingestion of raw, undercooked, or smoked meat or fish infected with tapeworm larvae can cause infection in humans. *T saginata* and *T solium* cysticerci are encysted in

Gastrointestinal Diseases

beef and pork and digested in the intestines where larvae are released. *D latum* plerocercoides live in the tissues of fish. They attach to the mucosa in the small intestine where they mature in 3 to 6 weeks. Adult tapeworms may survive in the human intestine for decades.

All tapeworms have a ribbon of segments (proglottids) produced constantly. Each proglottid develops into a self-contained hermaphroditic reproductive organism that produces large numbers of eggs and uses nutrients absorbed directly from the host's intestine. Mature adult worms comprise thousands of proglottids.

The mature proglottids of both *Taenia* species break off the distal end of the worm. Proglottids of *T solium* pass out of the host in the feces, and proglottids of *T saginata* force their way out through the anus. Yellow-brown *Taenia* eggs appear in the feces of some patients. In contrast, *D latum* proglottids daily excrete into the intestinal lumen approximately 1 million yellow-brown operculate eggs.

When cattle ingest *T saginata* eggs or proglottids or pigs ingest *T solium* eggs or proglottids in human feces, the embryos are digested out of the eggs in the intestine, penetrate the intestinal wall, and spread throughout the tissues. There they develop into mature infectious cysticerci within 10 weeks. The eggs of *T saginata* do not cause disease in humans, but the eggs of *T solium* do. Ingested *T solium* eggs may produce cysticerci in human subcutaneous tissues, brain, eyes, muscles, heart, liver, lungs, and peritoneum. Unwashed vegetables or fruits, such as strawberries, are particularly dangerous. Fecal contamination of hands may cause autoinfection. In some instances human cysticercosis results from consumption of eggs of dog tapeworms.

D latum eggs enter fresh water, develop into embryos, and hatch into ciliated, free-swimming coracidia. When minute crustacea ingest the coracidia, they develop into the elongated procercoid. Fish eat the crustacea, and the larvae penetrate the intestinal wall and lodge in the tissues where they grow and develop into mature infective plerocercoids. Humans ingest the plerocercoids in raw, rare, or smoked fish, and the adult tapeworms develop. Cooking and freezing destroy the infective organisms.

Beef and fish tapeworms are distributed worldwide; the pork tapeworm is less widespread. *T saginata* is most prevalent in East Africa and moderately prevalent in middle Europe, the Near East, and Central and South America. *T solium* is most prevalent in South Africa, Mexico, India,

the Slavic countries of Europe, Brazil, Chile, New Guinea, and northern China. *D latum* is most prevalent in Siberia, Canada, Argentina, Chile, the northern lake country of Scandinavia, northern Europe, and northern China. Humans are the only definitive hosts of the *T saginata* and *T solium* worms, and at least 22 mammal species are hosts for *D latum* worms. Most infected people have only one tapeworm.

Clinical characteristics and course

Passage in the feces of *T saginata* proglottids begins 10 to 14 weeks and passage of *T solium* proglottids begins 8 to 12 weeks after ingestion of eggs. Adult tapeworms usually do not cause problems in the human host because most humans harbor only one tapeworm. The most common symptom of *T saginata* infection is passage of motile proglottids through the anus. The weight produced by a *T saginata* worm in a year totals less than 2 pounds, an indication that those tapeworms do not consume significant quantities of the host's nutrients. However, *D latum* worms absorb large amounts of vitamin B_{12}, and worms that live high in the small intestine absorb enough of that essential vitamin to cause pernicious anemia in 1% to 2% of infected people.

Cysticercosis has an incubation period of 1 to many years. Human cysticercosis evolves unpredictably and differently in different patients. Death, often unexpected, can occur at any moment in patients with cysticerci in the nervous system. When cysticerci reach the brain, epilepsy and psychiatric disturbances may be the first signs of cysticercosis. In some patients, cysticerci can block the ventricular system of the brain, raise intracranial pressure, and thereby cause vomiting, violent headache, and visual disturbances.

Diagnosis

Tapeworms should be suspected when a patient passes motile proglottids of *T saginata* in the stool. Pernicious anemia may indicate that the patient has a *D latum* infection. A history of frequent ingestion of raw or undercooked meat is important in the diagnosis of tapeworms.

Feces can be concentrated before they are examined for *Taenia* eggs, and the Kato thick smear method is the simplest. The eggs of the two *Taenia* species cannot be differentiated, but the history of the patient's diet and the habitats and places visited may help with the diagnosis. Specific diagnosis is based on the morphology of the scoleces or gravid proglottids. Mature proglottids of the

Gastrointestinal Diseases

Taenia species can be pressed between two large glass slides and the lateral uterine segments counted. The large and characteristic eggs of *D latum* are easily detected in the feces.

Subcutaneous cysticerci are visible or palpable and may be identified after they are excised. The form of the scoleces determines the specific species. CAT scans or x-rays of the soft tissues may reveal calcified cysticerci; however, the organisms in the brain rarely calcify. Serologic testing is valuable.

Principles of treatment
Anthelmintics provide excellent results in treating tapeworm infections, and one appears to be efficacious for the treatment of cysticercosis.

Prevention
Immediate treatment of patients harboring adult *T solium* is essential to prevent cysticercosis. People infected with adult worms can reinfect themselves. To break the cycles involving humans and cattle or pigs, fecal contamination of soil, water, and human or animal food must be prevented. In particular, pigs must be prevented from having access to human feces. Beef and pork should be thoroughly cooked. Government inspection of meat prevents the sale of infected meat.

Selected reading

Brown WJ, Voge M: Cysticercosis. A modern day plague. *Pediatr Clin North Am* 1985;32:953-969.

Flisser A, Perez-Montfort R, Larralde C: The immunology of human and animal cysticercosis: A review. *Bull WHO* 1979;57:839-856.

Pawlowski Z, Schultz MG: Taeniasis and cysticercosis (*Taenia saginata*). *Adv Parasitol* 1972;10:269-343.

Richards FO Jr, Schantz PM, Ruiz-Tiben E, et al: Cysticercosis in Los Angeles County. *JAMA* 1985;254:3444-3448.

Saarni M, Nybergy W, Grasbeck R, et al: Symptoms in carriers of *Diphyllobothrium latum* and in non-infected controls. *Acta Med Scand* 1963;173:147-154.

Smyth JD, Heath DD: Pathogenesis of larval cestodes in mammals. *Helminth Abstr* 1970;39:1-22.

TROPICAL SPRUE

Agent
The agent is unknown but is thought to be one or more enteric organisms.

Distribution
See Figure 35.

Epidemiology
Tropical sprue is a form of malabsorption reported among visitors and indigenous persons in South America, the larger Caribbean islands, the Indian subcontinent, Southeast Asia, and Central America except Mexico. In some of those areas, prevalence rates among expatriates have been as high as 8%. Outbreaks follow a seasonal pattern and are closely related to epidemics of acute diarrhea. The duration of the stay in the tropics correlates with the risk of getting the disease.

Clinical characteristics and course
The incubation period is not well established although sprue has been diagnosed within 2 to 3 weeks after an episode of acute diarrhea. Onset may begin with 2 to 3 days of fever and malaise or insidiously, with diarrhea, weight loss, abdominal distention, and borborygmi. Colicky pain may occur; and stools may be voluminous, pale, and loose. Uncorrected sprue causes pallor, anemia, and protein-losing enteropathy, the complications of vitamin B_{12} and folic acid deficiencies.

Diagnosis
Villi in the small intestine are blunted, infiltrated to some degree with inflammatory cells, and scarred. Lactose and glucose tolerance test results are subnormal in a large proportion of patients with tropical sprue, and D-xylose absorption is reduced in all patients with the disease. Absorption of vitamin A and D is impaired, and folate and vitamin B_{12} blood concentrations are low. Steatorrhea occurs in 60% to 70% of patients. Absorption of amino acids and small peptides may be impaired.

Principles of treatment
Prolonged antibiotic therapy may reverse mild to moderate infections. Spontaneous resolution occurs in people who

Gastrointestinal Diseases

Figure 35. The distribution of tropical sprue.

Gastrointestinal Diseases

Genitourinary Diseases

remain in the tropics as well as in those who leave the tropics or change their diets. Folate and vitamin B_{12} therapy seem to restore appetite and weight gain and reverse anemia in a large proportion of patients. Prolonged folic acid therapy may be necessary.

Genitourinary Diseases to Consider in Travelers and Immigrants

SCHISTOSOMIASIS (See page 69)
SEXUALLY TRANSMITTED DISEASES

Prevention
If food is prepared hygienically during prolonged residence in tropical countries, the frequency of tropical sprue may decline. Good sanitation reduces the risk of sprue, and prophylaxis with oral antibiotics has substantially reduced the occurrence of the infection.

Selected reading

Aetiology and pathogenesis of tropical sprue: Do viruses play a role? *Trop Gastroenterol* 1985; 6:1-3.

Baker SJ: Tropical sprue. *Br Med Bull* 1972; 28:87-91.

Cook GC: *Tropical Gastroenterology.* New York, Oxford University Press, 1980, p 484.

Tomkins A: Tropical malabsorption: Recent concepts in pathogenesis and nutritional significance. *Clin Sci* 1981; 60:131-137.

Westergaard H: The sprue syndromes. *Am J Med Sci* 1985; 290:249-262.

Other Diseases to Consider in the Differential Diagnosis of Gastrointestinal Illness in Travelers and Immigrants

ANTHRAX (See page 82)
CAPILLARIASIS
ENTEROBIASIS
SCHISTOSOMIASIS (See page 69)
TOXOCARIASIS (See page 120)
TRICHURIASIS
YELLOW FEVER (See page 80)

Skin Diseases

LEISHMANIASIS, CUTANEOUS
(Aleppo, Baghdad or Delhi boil)

Agents
In the Eastern Hemisphere, the agents are *Leishmania donovani*, *Leishmania tropica*, *Leishmania major*, and *Leishmania aethiopica*; and in the Western Hemisphere, the agents are *Leishmania braziliensis* and *Leishmania mexicana*.

Distribution
See Figure 36.

Epidemiology
Leishmania are intracellular protozoan parasites transmitted among animals and between humans by sandflies of the genus *Phlebotomus*. *Leishmania* parasites exist in two different forms. In humans, the primary form is the oval or rounded amastigote. Sandflies take in amastigotes with a blood meal from infected people. The amastigotes change to spindle-shaped promastigotes in the fly's midgut, multiply, and extend to the foregut. When the sandfly bites, it transfers promastigotes to its mammalian victim.

Female sandfly vectors usually bite at night and hide in dark corners during the day. The insects are most abundant in dry areas of the tropics. Leishmaniasis is widespread throughout rural India and China; but in other regions, transmission may be focal and related to environmental changes. In many areas, the principal animal reservoir for the agents of cutaneous and visceral leishmaniases is the dog although gerbils and other wild rodents may be reservoirs.

Clinical characteristics and course
Eastern Hemisphere cutaneous leishmaniasis, also known as oriental sore, is distinguished by single or multiple lesions, which commonly occur on the face, arms, and legs and appear 2 to 8 weeks after the sandfly bites. Early lesions, small, erythematous papules 2 to 5 mm in diameter, slowly enlarge to a diameter of 1 to 2 cm. Within a few months, lesions can become ulcers that persist for up to 2 years and then slowly heal with scar formation. The ulcers can be dry and crusted or wet and oozing. Disseminated cutaneous leishmaniasis, apparently the result of depression or failure of the host's immune response, has been reported in a small proportion of patients in several areas where the disease is endemic.

In the Western Hemisphere, both cutaneous and mucocutaneous leishmaniases occur. Cutaneous lesions are similar to but are usually less nodular and less likely to form ulcers than lesions seen in the Eastern Hemisphere. The mucocutaneous lesions, also known as espundia, appear on the mucocutaneous borders of the nose and mouth and cause gross facial deformity. The lesions may appear from months to years after the primary lesion. The cartilaginous structures of the nose, palate, and larynx may be destroyed, and aspiration pneumonia or suffocation may be fatal. Patients who have had leishmaniasis acquire long-lasting immunity to the specific *Leishmania* species with which they were infected but no cross-immunity to other species.

Diagnosis
Skin nodules or ulcerating lesions suspected to be leishmaniasis can be diagnosed by examining scrapings from skin slit smears taken from the edges of ulcers. Several smears should be prepared, air dried, and stained with Giemsa stain. Leishman-Donovan bodies, or amastigotes, are visible within the macrophages. On special media, *Leishmania* can be cultured from aspirated material. Aspirated material injected into hamsters will produce characteristic skin lesions. A positive skin reaction to killed promastigotes provides presumptive evidence of infection. The agents that cause the different types of leishmaniasis cannot be differentiated morphologically. However, monoclonal antibodies and nucleic acid probes developed recently are helping to differentiate different species and strains.

Principles of treatment
Simple cutaneous lesions heal spontaneously in patients infected with certain *Leishmania* strains. Many patients with leishmaniasis require prolonged treatment with moderately toxic drugs. Pentavalent antimonial compounds and other antiprotozoal agents and antibiotics have been effective in the treatment of cutaneous leishmaniasis.

Prevention
The use of insect repellents and fine mesh netting may reduce the chances of being bitten by a sandfly. Sandflies have a short flight range and are highly susceptible to systematic spraying with residual insecticides.

Skin Diseases

Figure 36. The distribution of cutaneous leishmaniasis.

Skin Diseases

Selected reading

Freeman K: American cutaneous leishmaniasis. *J R Army Med Corps* 1983; 129:167-173.

Freeman K, deMello W: Leishmanin skin testing in the diagnosis of American cutaneous leishmaniasis. *Int J Dermatol* 1985;24:52-53.

Greenblatt CL: The present and future of vaccination for cutaneous leishmaniasis, in Mizrahi A (ed): *New Development with Human and Veterinary Vaccines.* New York, Alan R Liss, 1980, pp 259-285.

Neva FA: Diagnosis and treatment of cutaneous leishmaniasis, in Remington JS, Swartz MN (eds): *Current Clinical Topics in Infectious Diseases.* New York, McGraw-Hill Book Co, 1980, vol 3, pp 364-380.

Pearson RD, Wheeler DA, Harrison LH, et al: The immunobiology of leishmaniasis. *Rev Infect Dis* 1983; 5:907-927.

Schewach-Millet M, Kahana M, Ronnen M, et al: Mucosal involvement of cutaneous leishmaniasis. *Int J Dermatol* 1986; 25:113-114.

YAWS AND PINTA
(Frambesia tropica, pian, and caraate)

Agents
Treponema pertenue (yaws)
Treponema carateum (pinta)

Distribution
See Figure 37.

Epidemiology
The spirochetes that cause yaws and pinta are transmitted through broken skin after close contact with infected people. The diseases are most prevalent in rural tropical areas where hygiene is poor and living conditions are crowded. Yaws occurs most often in 2- to 5-year olds, and pinta occurs most often in older children and adolescents. During global campaigns in the 1950s and 1960s, yaws and pinta were nearly eradicated; but their prevalence is increasing in the absence of control efforts.

Clinical characteristics and course
Yaws. After an incubation period of 2 weeks to 3 months, a papilloma appears on the face, arms, or legs and persists for weeks or months. The lesion expands slowly to form multiple papillomatous, or raspberry, lesions, which may ulcerate in the center. The primary papillomas heal spontaneously within months. Secondary papillomas may erupt, heal, and spread in successive crops; and painful papillomas and hyperkeratoses may appear on the palms or soles. The secondary lesions may be associated with lymphadenopathy, and osteitis and periosteitis can destroy the long bones. A variety of skin lesions can appear in the late stage of the disease with gummatous lesions at several sites. Yaws cripples and deforms but is rarely fatal.

Pinta. One to eight weeks after infection, a scaling papule appears on hands, legs, face, or dorsum of the feet. The papule may be accompanied by lymphadenitis. In 3 to 12 months, a maculopapular erythematous rash appears at the sites of the primary lesions; it may change color from blue to violet to brown and finally become depigmented. The rash and pigmented lesions can recur for years, and the depigmented lesions can cause considerable disfigurement.

Diagnosis
Spirochetes can be found in early skin lesions of patients with either disease. Serologic tests for syphilis become positive during the early stages of either infection.

Principles of treatment
Small doses of an antibiotic cure both diseases.

Prevention
Improved sanitation, including increased use of soap and water, will prevent transmission. Case finding and antibiotic treatment control the diseases.

Selected reading

Antal GM, Causse G: The control of endemic treponematoses. *Rev Infect Dis* 1985; 7(suppl 2):S220-S226.

Brown ST: Therapy for nonvenereal treponematoses. Review of the efficiency of penicillin and consideration of alternatives. *Rev Infect Dis* 1985; 7(suppl 2):S318-S326.

Green CA, Harman RR: Yaws truly – A survey of patients indexed under 'yaws' and a review of clinical and laboratory problems of diagnosis. *Clin Exp Dermatol* 1986; 11:41-48.

Vorst FA: Clinical diagnosis and changing manifestations of treponemal infection. *Rev Infect Dis* 1985;7(suppl 2):S327-S331.

Skin Diseases

Figure 37. The distribution of yaws and pinta.

●●●● Pinta
●●●● Yaws

Skin Diseases

Other Diseases or Circumstances to Consider in the Differential Diagnosis of Skin Diseases in Travelers and Immigrants

ANTHRAX (See page 82)
BLASTOMYCOSIS
ENTEROVIRAL SYNDROMES
LEPROSY (See page 59)
LYME DISEASE
MEASLES
RUBELLA
SCABIES
SCHISTOSOMIASIS (See page 69)
TOXOCARIASIS (See page 120)
TYPHUS FEVERS (See page 78)
VARICELLA
VENOMOUS BITES OR STINGS

Neuromuscular Diseases

GNATHOSTOMIASIS

Agent
Gnathostoma spinigerum

Distribution
See Figure 38.

Epidemiology
Adult *Gnathostoma* worms attach to the walls of the intestines of dogs and cats. The granulomatous tissue that forms in response surrounds the worms but leaves an opening for nutrition and egg deposition. Eggs are excreted in feces. In water, the eggs hatch into first-stage larvae, which are ingested by freshwater cyclopes, which in turn are eaten by several species of freshwater fish. In the fish, third-stage larvae develop and can parasitize a wide spectrum of vertebrate species. In Thailand, for example, domestic chickens and ducks fed waste fish are infected. Larvae penetrate the gastric mucosa and the liver and eventually migrate through the circulatory system to muscles. Humans who eat undercooked, infected fowl or fish are infected with third-stage larvae and become incidental transfer hosts. The larvae migrate to the muscles, usually in the arms or legs, and in a few patients to the eye or the central nervous system. When dogs or cats eat third-stage larvae, the worms mature, mate, and continue the cycle.

Clinical characteristics and course
A few days after infection, patients experience fever, vomiting, and abdominal pain. Two to four weeks later, diffuse redness and swelling ranging from the size of a plum to the size of a grapefruit appear, usually on one arm or leg. The swelling may migrate to some other site, or it may disappear and then reappear at the original site. *Gnathostoma* larvae emerge from the skin of some patients. At times the patient may have no signs, or the swelling may cause deep, dull pain in muscles. In rare patients, the larvae enter the eye, brain, or spinal cord, where they cause severe pain and local central nervous system signs and symptoms. In all patients with gnathostomiasis, symptoms persist for 2 to 5 years, rarely longer.

Diagnosis
Leukocytosis is mild to moderate with 10% to 96% eosinophils. The diagnosis of gnathostomiasis is likely if the patient reacts positively to a skin test made from larval antigens or if antibodies increase as measured by an ELISA or a radioimmunoassay.

Principles of treatment
No chemotherapeutic agent is known to be effective, but the worms can sometimes be removed surgically.

Prevention
In places where the disease is endemic, consumption of "fermented," undercooked, or raw fowl or freshwater fish should be avoided.

Selected reading

Chitanondh H, Rosen L: Fatal eosinophilic encephalomyelitis caused by the nematode *Gnathostoma spinigerum. Am J Trop Med Hyg* 1967;16:638-645.

Dharmkrong-at A, Migasena S, Suntharasamai P, et al: Enzyme-linked immunosorbent assay for detection of antibody to *Gnathostoma* antigen in patients with intermittent cutaneous migratory swelling. *J Clin Microbiol* 1986; 23:47-51.

Other Diseases to Consider in the Differential Diagnosis of Neuromuscular Diseases in Travelers and Immigrants

LYME DISEASE
POLIOMYELITIS

Neuromuscular Diseases

Figure 38. The distribution of gnathostomiasis.

Ophthalmic Diseases

TOXOCARIASIS
(Visceral larva migrans)

Agents
Toxocara canis and *Toxocara cati*

Distribution
Worldwide

Epidemiology
Dogs, cats, and foxes harbor mature adult *Toxocara* roundworms in the small intestine. Each worm releases eggs which embryonate in the soil. In the dog, eggs hatch in the small intestine and larvae enter the portal veins and are carried to the liver, heart, and lungs. The larvae migrate to many organs and tissues and encyst. Uterine cysts are broken down during pregnancy, and migrating larvae infect puppies in utero and are excreted from the mammary glands in the milk. In puppies, larvae enter alveoli, migrate up the trachea, are swallowed, and establish or augment intestinal infection.

Humans are infected by ingesting embryonated eggs in soil or feces. Eggs hatch in the proximal small intestine, and larvae migrate throughout the body. They produce hemorrhagic necrosis, inflammation, and granulomatous lesions. Fewer than 20% of infections occur in adults. Most infections in humans are in toddlers who eat dirt. A sandbox used as a defecation site by dogs or cats is particularly hazardous.

Clinical characteristics and course
Most infected humans do not have an overt disease. Their infections can cause mild eosinophilia or low titers of antibody to *Toxocara*.

Overt disease has two forms, ocular larva migrans, more common in older than in younger children, and visceral larva migrans, more common in younger than in older children. In patients with ocular larva migrans, *Toxocara* produce a granuloma resembling a retinoblastoma. The lesion causes leukokoria, strabismus, failing vision, a mass in the fundus, and endophthalmitis. Larvae may cause an eosinophilic abscess in any portion of the eye.

In patients with visceral larva migrans, clinical signs include fever, wheezing or coughing, and hepatomegaly; and chest x-ray film may show pulmonary infiltrates. Laboratory findings include persistent eosinophilia, leukocytosis, and hypergammaglobulinemia. Rarely, larvae may migrate to the central nervous system, where they can trigger seizures. *Toxocara* infections may contribute to childhood asthma by mechanisms that are not completely understood.

Diagnosis
Ocular larva migrans may be difficult to distinguish from other childhood ocular diseases. Antibodies that appear in the vitreous humor may be detected by an ELISA.

A presumptive diagnosis of visceral larva migrans is based on clinical signs, laboratory findings, and a history of eating dirt or exposure to puppies. Several serologic tests are available. An ELISA using larval antigens may be quite accurate; but first, sera should be adsorbed with *Ascaris* antigens because *Toxocara* and *Ascaris* share many antigens. A skin test is used widely but may give false-positive results in patients with concurrent *Ascaris* infections.

Principles of treatment
Visceral larva migrans is usually self-limited. Antilarval or anthelmintic agents have cured some patients, but theoretically antilarval therapy could be inappropriate. Anti-inflammatory agents are highly effective in certain patients. Because a single larva may produce severe visual loss, prompt diagnosis and treatment are essential for a good prognosis. Laser therapy has also been used.

Prevention
Canine and feline feces should be removed from children's play areas, particularly from sandboxes. Cats and dogs should be wormed at 3 weeks of age and then at 2-week intervals for three treatments and every 6 months thereafter. Parents should be educated about the hazards of eating dirt and of exposure to puppies and dogs.

Selected reading
Bruckner DA: Serologic and intradermal tests for parasitic infections. *Pediatr Clin North Am* 1985;32:1063-1075.

Elliot DL, Tolle SW, Goldberg L, et al: Pet-associated illness. *N Engl J Med* 1985;313:985-995.

Glickman LT, Schantz PM: Epidemiology and pathogenesis of zoonotic toxocariasis. *Epidemiol Rev* 1981;3:230-250.

Roth RM, Gleckman RA: Human infections derived from dogs. *Postgrad Med* 1985;77:169-173, 176-178, 180.

Ophthalmic Diseases

TRACHOMA

Agent
Chlamydia trachomatis

Distribution
See Figure 39.

Epidemiology
Trachoma is a disease caused by long-term untreated chlamydial infections of the conjunctivae of people living in poor, crowded conditions. It is the primary cause of preventable blindness. The development of the disease may be related to the host's characteristics such as malnutrition and a history of repeated infections and to the microorganism's characteristics such as differences in the virulence of various chlamydial strains. In people living in good socioeconomic circumstances, the same microorganisms seldom produce the complete trachoma syndrome.

Trachoma is transmitted by personal contact and flies, especially *Musca sorbens*, that feed on conjunctival discharges. The disease commonly begins in young children who may transmit it on their fingers. Sexual transmission of the microorganism with autoinoculation of the conjunctivae occurs in a large proportion of patients. Exposure to dry winds, dust, and fine sand may contribute to the severity of disease.

Clinical characteristics and course
Conjunctivitis begins insidiously 5 to 12 days after infection and is characterized by bilateral conjunctival inflammation, lymphoid follicles, and papillary hyperplasia. Typically patients have no systemic signs or symptoms. Untreated trachoma becomes chronic with spontaneous remissions and exacerbations. Weeks or months later, blood vessels form in the upper half of the cornea and produce a fibrovascular pannus that impairs vision. That process is followed by conjunctival scarring, decreased lacrimation, deformity of the eyelids, infections of the cornea, corneal opacity, and blindness. Bacterial infection contributes to scar formation.

Diagnosis
Soon after infection, *Chlamydia* can be recovered from conjunctival scrapings and stained with Giemsa stain or identified with a febrile agglutinins test using specific antisera.

Treatment
Antibiotics applied topically to the eye and administered systemically when indicated cure trachoma. Eyelid scarring may require surgical correction.

Prevention
Fly control and good sanitation are helpful. Early recognition and treatment of trachoma are essential parts of any program of prevention. No effective vaccine exists, but prophylactic antibiotics prevent infection in people who are contacts of infected patients.

Selected reading

Dawson CR, Jones BR, Tarizzo ML: *Program for the Prevention of Blindness. Guide to Trachoma Control.* Geneva, World Health Organization, 1981.

Fraunfelder FT, Roy FH: *Current Ocular Therapy.* Philadelphia, WB Saunders Co, 1980.

Jones BR: Changing concepts of trachoma and its control. *Trans Ophthalmol Soc UK* 1980;100:25-29.

Pruessner HT, Hansel NK, Griffiths M: Diagnosis and treatment of chlamydial infections. *Am Fam Physician* 1986;34:81-92.

Other Diseases to Consider in the Differential Diagnosis of Ophthalmic Diseases in Travelers and Immigrants

CONJUNCTIVITIS, ACUTE HEMORRHAGIC
FILARIASES (See page 50, loiasis and onchocerciasis)
LEPROSY (See page 59)

Ophthalmic Diseases

Figure 39. The distribution of trachoma.

Central Nervous System Diseases

ANGIOSTRONGYLIASIS
(Eosinophilic meningoencephalitis or meningitis)

Agent
Angiostrongylus cantonensis

Distribution
See Figure 40.

Epidemiology
Various species of rats are the definitive hosts. They are infected when they eat third-stage larvae in snails, slugs, or land planarians. The larvae migrate to the brain, mature to the adult stage, and then migrate through the nervous system to the pulmonary arteries. There, adult worms mate, and eggs hatch; larvae migrate into the bronchial system, pass up the trachea, and are swallowed and passed in the feces. Mollusks, the intermediate hosts, are infected with first-stage larvae that mature to a third stage.

Humans are infected by eating raw or undercooked land snails or prawns, fish, or land crabs that have ingested snails or slugs and transport larvae. Lettuce and other leafy vegetables may be contaminated by slugs or snails. Children can be infected when playing around snail slime trails. Humans enter the parasite's life cycle accidentally, and the cycle stops.

Clinical characteristics and course
Most human infections are subclinical. After an incubation period of 1 to 3 weeks, the larval nematode may have migrated to the central nervous system of the human host. The host's symptoms of angiostrongyliasis include low grade fever, severe headache, stiffness of the back and neck, various paresthesias, and possibly facial paralysis. Some patients also have vomiting, diminished visual acuity, and cranial nerve palsies. The illness may last from days to months and usually resolves without treatment.

Diagnosis
No specific tests identify the infection. In the cerebrospinal fluid (CSF), white blood cells increase, and 25% to 100% of the cells may be eosinophils; but the blood may not contain excess eosinophils. Therefore the human infection has been called eosinophilic meningitis. The worm is found in the CSF or the eye of some patients.

Principles of treatment
No specific treatment exists.

Prevention
In areas where *A cantonensis* is endemic, raw foods, including land snails, should not be eaten. Boiling snails, prawns, fish, and crabs for 3 to 5 minutes or freezing at 15°C for 24 hours kills the larvae. Good personal hygiene is also important in prevention.

Selected reading

Alicata JE, Jindrak K: *Angiostrongyliasis in the Pacific and Southeast Asia.* Springfield, IL, Charles C Thomas, 1970.

Punyagupta S, Juttijudata P, Bunnag T: Eosinophilic meningitis in Thailand. Clinical studies of 484 typical cases probably caused by *Angiostrongylus cantonensis. Am J Trop Med Hyg* 1975;24:921-931.

Rosen L, Loison G, Laigret J, et al: Studies on eosinophilic meningitis. Epidemiologic and clinical observations on Pacific Islands and the possible etiologic role of *Angiostrongylus cantonensis. Am J Epidemiol* 1967; 85:17-44.

Yii CY: Clinical observations on eosinophilic meningitis and meningoencephalitis caused by *Angiostrongylus cantonensis* on Taiwan. *Am J Trop Med Hyg* 1976;25:233-243.

CRYPTOCOCCOSIS
(Torulosis, European blastomycosis)

Agent
Cryptococcus neoformans (*Filobasidiella neoformans* is the sexual, or perfect, form.)

Distribution
Worldwide

Epidemiology
The fungus grows in soil usually infected by the excretions of pigeons with enteric infections. Humans are usually resistant unless they are aged, suffering from an immune deficiency disorder such as AIDS, or taking immunosuppressive agents. Cryptococcosis is transmitted by airborne spores that are inhaled. It occurs sporadically throughout

Central Nervous System Diseases

Figure 40. The distribution of angiostrongyliais.

Central Nervous System Diseases

the world, particularly in people with unusually frequent exposure to pigeons or pigeon droppings.

Clinical characteristics and course
The incubation period is not known but probably ranges from months to years. A silent pulmonary infection has usually preceded meningeal invasion. Commonly patients with cryptococcosis first complain of headaches that are caused by meningitis. Other signs are blurred vision, confusion, depression, agitation, or inappropriate speech or dress. Typically, protein and cell counts in the cerebrospinal fluid (CSF) are abnormal, and glucose concentration is decreased. The kidney is the next most common organ involved. The organism can be cultivated from urine in 30% of patients. Skin and mucous membrane, bone, prostate, and adrenal infections occur rarely.

Diagnosis
With high, dry magnification, the budding yeast surrounded by a clear capsule is visible in CSF, urine, and sputum to which India ink has been added. The fungus can be isolated from cultures of the same fluids and exudates. No skin test exists.

Principles of treatment
Certain antibiotics are moderately effective in patients with cryptococcal meningitis; combination therapy is sometimes appropriate. Skin, bone, and renal infections require therapy; but asymptomatic lung infections do not.

Prevention
Large accumulations of pigeon droppings should be removed and decontaminated before disposal.

Selected reading

Baes H, VanOutsem J: Primary cutaneous cryptococcosis. *Dermatologica* 1985;171:357-361.

Lyons RW, Andriole VT: Fungal infections of the CNS. *Neurol Clin* 1986; 4:159-170.

Sabetta JR, Andriole VT: Cryptococcal infection of the central nervous system. *Med Clin North Am* 1985;69:333-344.

Scholer HJ: Diagnosis of cryptococcosis and monitoring of chemotherapy. *Mykosen* 1985;28:5-16.

RABIES
(Hydrophobia, lyssa)

Agent
Rabies virus

Distribution
See Figure 41.

Epidemiology
Rabies occurs in urban as well as rural areas. In Europe, the United States, and Canada, rabies principally infects wild animals, eg, raccoons, skunks, and foxes. Bites from or contact with infected wild animals infects humans. Bites from infected fructivorous or insectivorous bats also transmit the disease but only rarely. In Central America, northern South America, some Caribbean islands, and parts of Mexico, vampire bats transmit rabies to domestic animals and to a few humans. In most developing countries, the rabies virus is enzootic in domestic and feral dogs and cats. Human infections usually result from bites by animals with the signs of rabies, but animals without signs of rabies can transmit the disease.

Clinical characteristics and course
The incubation period may be as short as 10 days, is usually 2 to 8 weeks, but in a few patients is a few months to a year. Rabies begins with abnormal sensations at the site of the bite, fever, headache, malaise, and a sense of apprehension. Over a few days, rabies progresses in the central nervous system and produces varying degrees of paralysis and behavioral changes. Attempts to swallow cause severe, painful spasms of the muscles of the pharynx or larynx. Eventually patients have convulsions, severe paralysis, and sometimes delirium. Untreated patients become comatose and shortly thereafter die following respiratory arrest. Three patients have survived following intensive treatment.

Diagnosis
A history of exposure can be the key to the diagnosis. No tests will diagnose rabies in humans before symptoms begin. Specific inclusion bodies can be identified in brain or salivary gland tissue with a fluorescent antibody test. The virus can be isolated in tissue cultures or mice inoculated with brain or salivary gland tissue or other tissues or fluids

Central Nervous System Diseases

Figure 41. The distribution of the rabies virus.

Central Nervous System Diseases

from a patient. Viral antigen can be identified in dermal, corneal, or mucosal scrapings. With neutralization or complement fixation tests or an ELISA, a rise in antibody titers can be measured in paired sera.

Principles of treatment

Prevention before or after exposure is more important than treatment although a few patients who have been treated in intensive care units have recovered from rabies. Animal bites should be cleansed with soap or detergent and debrided when necessary. Rabies immune globulin should be inoculated into and around bites that penetrate tissues. That treatment is particularly important for patients with head wounds from wild animals, dogs, or cats with rabies symptoms. Immune serum globulin is almost always given with rabies vaccine. If the probability of rabies is low because the animal that bit the patient does not appear to be rabid or the patient has been immunized, only the vaccine is given. The most efficacious rabies vaccine available is made in human or monkey cell cultures and can be administered in five divided doses given intramuscularly or intradermally over 28 days.

Prevention

The most important means of rabies prevention is control of the disease in domestic animals. After that are wound care and immunoprophylaxis described in the treatment section above. Rabies can also be prevented before exposure. People who live for prolonged periods in areas where rabies is enzootic should be immunized. Serum antibody titers should be measured, and an additional injection of vaccine given if the titers are inadequate. Antibody titers of people at continuing risk should be measured at 2-year intervals and the prophylaxis repeated as needed.

Selected reading

Field evaluation of pre-exposure use of human diploid cell rabies vaccine. *MMWR* 1983;32:601-603.

Maton PN, Pollard JD, Davis JN: Human rabies encephalomyelitis. *Br Med J* 1976;1:1038-1040.

Morrison AJ Jr, Wenzel RP: Rabies: A review and current approach for the clinician. *South Med J* 1985;78:1211-1218.

Rabies prevention – United States, 1984. *MMWR* 1984;33:393-402, 407-408.

Rest JG, Goldstein EJ: Management of human and animal bite wounds. *Emerg Clin North Am* 1985;3:117-126.

TETANUS
(Lockjaw)

Agent
Clostridium tetani

Distribution
Worldwide

Epidemiology

Tetanus is transmitted when spores in soil, dust, and human or animal feces get into a puncture wound, a laceration, or a burn; grow in the anaerobic conditions; and produce a neurotoxic exotoxin. Most tetanus spores are found in agricultural regions of developing countries where animals and humans share the same habitat. Tetanus may also be a complication of the parenteral and subcutaneous use of illicit drugs.

Clinical characteristics and course

The incubation period may be as short as 1 to 2 days or as long as 1 month but averages 10 days. Patients with mild tetanus suffer from general or local muscle rigidity, especially the muscles of the jaw, face, neck, and back. Classically, however, patients experience abdominal rigidity and painful muscle contractions of the neck and jaw, typically caused by sensory stimuli. Spasms produce opisthotonus and risus sardonicus, a grin. In some patients antagonistic muscles stiffen. Trismus is the cardinal sign. Severe tetanus causes intense muscle spasms that may fracture vertebrae, prevent ventilation, or cause autonomic disturbances. Most but not all patients have a history of injury. Fatality rates vary from 30% to 90% depending on the patient's age, stage of illness when treatment began, and form of treatment.

Diagnosis

Specific diagnosis of tetanus is rarely possible. Diagnosis is based on the clinical and epidemiologic features of the infection.

Central Nervous System Diseases

Principles of treatment

Treatment is essentially symptomatic. The wound is debrided to remove the bacteria that produce the exotoxin, and tetanus immune globulin (human origin antitoxin) is given intramuscularly or intravenously. Antibiotics, sedatives, and muscle relaxants should be administered as needed; and the patient's airway must be kept open. Before tetanus antitoxin of animal origin is used, hypersensitivity should be determined by intradermal inoculation. Active immunization should also be initiated.

Prevention

The first principle of prevention is adequate immunization with tetanus toxoid early in life and subsequent booster injections at 10-year intervals. Wounds should be carefully debrided, and the patient should be treated with appropriate antibiotics. A toxoid booster injection should be given if the last booster was given more than 5 years before. Tetanus immune globulin and toxoid should be given at different sites if the wound was not clean and the patient has not had the full series of immunization injections.

Selected reading

Diphtheria, tetanus, and pertussis: Guidelines for vaccine prophylaxis and other preventative measures. Recommendation of the Immunization Practices Advisory Committee. Centers for Disease Control, Department of Health and Human Services. *Ann Intern Med* 1985;103:896-905.

Dowell VR Jr: Botulism and tetanus: Selected epidemiologic and microbiologic aspects. *Rev Infect Dis* 1984;6 (suppl 1):S202-S207.

Holloway WJ, Reinhardt JF: Infectious disease emergencies. *Primary Care* 1986;13:119-134.

Mellanby J, Green J: How does tetanus toxin act? *Neuroscience* 1981; 6:281-300.

Relyveld EH: Current developments in production and testing of tetanus and diphtheria vaccines. *Prog Clin Biol Res* 1980;47:51-76.

Stanfield JP, Galaska A: Neonatal tetanus in the world today. *Bull WHO* 1984; 62:647-669.

Other Diseases to Consider in the Differential Diagnosis of Central Nervous System Diseases in Travelers and Immigrants

COCCIDIOIDOMYCOSIS
CYSTICERCOSIS (See page 108)
DIPHTHERIA
ENTEROVIRAL SYNDROMES
GNATHOSTOMIASIS (See page 118)
LEPROSY (See page 59)
LEPTOSPIROSIS (See page 62)
LYME DISEASE
MALARIA (See page 62)
MENINGITIS, MENINGOCOCCAL
MENINGOENCEPHALITIS, PRIMARY AMEBIC
PARAGONIMIASIS (See page 83)
SCHISTOSOMIASIS (See page 69)
TOXOCARIASIS (See page 120)
TRYPANOSOMIASIS, AFRICAN (See page 73)

Appendix

SOURCES OF INFORMATION ABOUT THE DIAGNOSIS AND MANAGEMENT OF DISEASES OF TRAVELERS AND IMMIGRANTS

Management of Highly Infectious Diseases

(eg, Lassa fever, Ebola-Marburg disease, Congo-Crimean hemorrhagic fever, Rift Valley fever)

Publications

Centers for Disease Control. Interstate shipment of etiologic agents. *Federal Register* 1980; 45:48626-48629. (US Dept of Health and Human Services publication No. 42 CFR, pt 72. Atlanta, Centers for Disease Control.)

Centers for Disease Control. Recommendations for initial management of suspected or confirmed cases of Lassa fever. *MMWR* 1980;28(suppl):18-125.

Centers for Disease Control. Viral hemorrhagic fever: Initial management of suspected and confirmed cases. *MMWR* 1983; 32(suppl 2):27S-38S.

Garner JS, Simmons BP: Centers for Disease Control. Guideline for isolation precautions in hospitals. *Infect Control* 1983;4:245-325.

Mitchell SW, McCormick JB: *Mobile Clinical Laboratory Manual. Clinical Laboratory Support for the Management of Patients Suspected of Infection with Class IV Agents.* Atlanta, Centers for Disease Control, 1982, pp 1-60.

Telephone numbers at the Center for Infectious Diseases, Centers for Disease Control

Chief, Special Pathogens Branch 404-329-3867
Medical Epidemiologist 404-329-3588
Director, Division of Viral Diseases 404-329-3091
Office of Biosafety 404-329-3883
Weekends or nights 404-329-2888
General number at the CDC 404-329-3311

Travel medicine clinics

Travel medicine clinics, also called geographic medicine or tropical medicine clinics, are housed at academic medical centers in major cities, particularly on the coasts. Patients can be referred for pretravel counseling, diagnosis, and management; laboratory specimens can be submitted for identification; and clinic staff members will consult with private physicians about diseases of immigrants and travelers. Some of the clinics are listed below.

Section of Infectious Diseases
Department of Medicine
University of Arizona School of Medicine
1501 North Campbell Avenue
Tucson, AZ 85724

Travelers' Clinic
University Hospital
San Diego, CA 92110

Overseas Medical Center
10 California Street
San Francisco, CA 94111

The Immunization Center
18411 Clark Street
Tarzana, CA 91356

Infectious Disease Division
Department of Medicine
University of Colorado Health Science Center
4200 East Ninth Avenue
Denver, CO 80262

Travel Medicine-International Travel Clinic
Yale University School of Medicine
20 York Street
New Haven, CT 06510

Travelers' Medical Service of Washington
2141 K Street NW
Washington, DC 20006

Tropical Medicine and Travelers' Clinic
1750 Northeast 168th Street
Room 318
North Miami Beach, FL 33162

Department of Infectious Diseases
Rush-Presbyterian-St. Luke's Medical Center
1753 West Congress Parkway
Chicago, IL 60612

Travel Clinic
University of Chicago Hospitals & Clinics
5841 South Maryland
Chicago, IL 60637

Travel Immunization Center
Northwestern Memorial Hospital
250 East Superior Street, Suite 168
Chicago, IL 60611

Travelers' Clinic
Department of Tropical Medicine
Tulane Medical Center Hospital
1430 Tulane Avenue
New Orleans, LA 70112

Medical Advisory Service for Travelers
Hampton House B139
Johns Hopkins Medical Institutions
624 North Broadway
Baltimore, MD 21205

Logan Airport Medical Station of the Massachusetts General Hospital
Logan International Airport
Boston, MA 02128

Travelers' Clinic
New England Medical Center
171 Harrison Avenue
Boston, MA 02118

Executive Health Examiners Intermedic
777 Third Avenue
New York, NY 10017

International Health Care Services of New York
440 East 69th Street
New York, NY 10021

Travelers' Clinic
Division of Geographic Medicine
University Hospital
2058 Abington Road
Cleveland, OH 44106

Immunization Service
University of Pennsylvania Hospital
34th & Spruce Streets
Philadelphia, PA 19103

Travelers' Health Center
Medical College of Pennsylvania
3300 Henry Avenue
Philadelphia, PA 19129

Geographic Medicine Program in Infectious Diseases
University of Texas Health Service Center
6431 Fannin
Texas Medical Center
Houston, TX 77025

Center for Infectious Diseases
Microbiology and Immunology
University of Utah School of Medicine
Salt Lake City, UT 84132

Travelers' Clinic
University of Virginia
Division of Geographic Medicine
Box 485
School of Medicine
Charlottesville, VA 22908

Travel and Tropical Medicine Clinic
University of Washington
University Hospital
1959 NE Pacific Street
Seattle, WA 98195

Travelers' Clinic
Toronto General Hospital
567 University Avenue
Toronto, Ontario
Canada

Centre for Tropical Diseases
The Montreal General Hospital
1650 Cedar
Room 787
Montreal, Quebec HeG 1A4
Canada

State departments of health

A valuable source of diagnostic consultation, laboratory support, and information about vaccinations and reporting diseases is the State Epidemiologist. Consultations are best done by telephone; however, because the telephone numbers change frequently, they are not listed here.

Alabama Department of Public Health
206 State Office Building
Montgomery, AL 36130

Alaska Division of Public Health
Pouch H-06H
Juneau, AK 99811

Arizona Department of Health Services
1740 West Adams Street
Phoenix, AZ 85007

Arkansas Department of Health
4815 West Markham
Little Rock, AR 72201

California Department of Health Services
714/744 P Street
Sacramento, CA 95814

Colorado Department of Health
4210 East 11th Avenue
Denver, CO 80220

State of Connecticut Department of Health Services
79 Elm Street
Hartford, CT 06106

Delaware Division of Public Health
Capitol Square
Dover, DE 19901

District of Columbia Department of Human Services
1875 Connecticut Avenue, NW
Washington, DC 20009

Florida Department of Health
1317 Winewood Boulevard
Building 6, Room 276
Tallahassee, FL 32301

Georgia Department of Human Resources
2 Martin Luther King Jr Drive
12th Floor
Atlanta, GA 30334

Guam Department of Public Health & Social Services
PO Box 2816
Government of Guam
Agana, GU 96910

Hawaii State Department of Health
PO Box 3378
Honolulu, HI 96801

Idaho Department of Health and Welfare
Statehouse Mail
Boise, ID 83720

Illinois Department of Public Health
535 West Jefferson
Springfield, IL 62761

Indiana State Board of Health
1330 West Michigan Street
PO Box 1964
Indianapolis, IN 46206

Iowa State Department of Health
Lucas State Office Building
3rd Floor
Des Moines, IA 50319

Kansas Department of Health and Environment
Forbes Field
Building 321
Topeka, KS 66620

Kentucky Department of Human Resources
275 East Main Street
Frankfort, KY 40621

Louisiana Office of Health Services and Environmental Quality
325 Loyola Avenue
Room 304
New Orleans, LA 70112

Maine Department of Human Services
Bureau of Health
State House Station #11
Augusta, ME 04333

Mariana Islands Department of Health Services
Trust Territory of the Pacific Islands
Office of the High Commissioner
Saipan, Mariana Islands 96950

Maryland Department of Health and Mental Hygiene
300 West Preston Street
Baltimore, MD 21201

Massachusetts Department of Public Health
600 Washington Street
Boston, MA 02111

Michigan Department of Public Health
3500 North Logan
PO Box 30035
Lansing, MI 48909

Minnesota Department of Health
717 Delaware Street, SE
Minneapolis, MN 55440

Mississippi State Board of Health
PO Box 1700
Jackson, MS 39205

Missouri Division of Health
PO Box 570
Jefferson City, MO 65102

Montana Department of Health and Environmental Sciences
Cogswell Building
Helena, MT 59620

State of Nebraska
Department of Health
301 Centennial Mall South
PO Box 95007
Lincoln, NE 68509

Nevada Department of Human Resources
Room 200, Kinhead Building
505 East King Street
Carson City, NV 89710

New Hampshire Division of Public Health
Health and Welfare Building
Hazen Drive
Concord, NH 03301

New Jersey Department of Health
John Fitch Plaza, CN 364
Trenton, NJ 08625

New Mexico Health and Environmental Department
PO Box 968
Santa Fe, NM 87504

New York State Health Department
Tower Building
Room 1084
Empire State Plaza
Albany, NY 12237

North Carolina Department of Human Resources
PO Box 2091
Raleigh, NC 27602

North Dakota State Health Department
Capitol Building
Bismarck, ND 58505

Ohio Department of Health
246 North High Street
PO Box 118
Columbus, OH 43216

Oklahoma Department of Health
NE 10th and Stonewall
Oklahoma City, OK 73152

Oregon Department of Human Resources
508 State Office Building
1400 SE 5th
PO Box 231
Portland, OR 97207

Pennsylvania Department of Health
PO Box 90
Harrisburg, PA 17108

Puerto Rico Department of Health
San Juan, PR 00908

Rhode Island Department of Health
103 Cannon Building
75 Davis Street
Providence, RI 02908

South Carolina Department of Health and Environmental Control
2600 Bull Street
Columbia, SC 29201

State of South Dakota Health Department
523 East Capitol
Pierre, SD 57501

Tennessee State Department of Health
State Office Building
Ben Alles Road
Nashville, TN 37216

Texas Department of Health
1100 West 49th Street
Austin, TX 78756

Utah Department of Health
PO Box 2500
Salt Lake City, UT 84110

Vermont State Health Department
60 Main Street
Burlington, VT 05401

Virginia State Health Department
Room 100
109 Governor Street
Richmond, VA 23219

Virgin Islands Department of Health
PO Box 520
Christiansted
St Croix, USVI 00820

Washington Department of Social and Health Services
Mail Stop LB12C
Olympia, WA 98504

West Virginia Department of Health
1800 Washington Street
Room 535
Charleston, WV 25305

Wisconsin State Health Department
PO Box 309
Madison, WI 53701

Wyoming Department of Health and Social Services
Hathaway Building
4th Floor
Cheyenne, WY 82002

Agencies of the Federal Government in the United States

Traveler's Medical Service of Washington
US State Department
Washington, DC 20037

Overseas Citizens Emergency Center
US State Department
Washington, DC 20037

Medical Epidemiologist
Centers for Disease Control
Atlanta, GA 30333

Drug Service
Centers for Disease Control
US Public Health Service
Atlanta, GA 30333

Vaccination Requirements

International Health Regulations (1969), Third Annotated Edition. Geneva, World Health Organization, 1983.

Vaccination Certificate Requirements. Situation as of 1 January 1985. And Health Advice for International Travel. Geneva, World Health Organization, 1985.

The following publications outline the recommendations of the Public Health Service Advisory Committee on Immunization Practices (ACIP):

Adult immunization: Recommendations of the Immunization Practices Advisory Committee (ACIP). *MMWR* 1984;33(suppl 1):1S-68S.

General recommendations on immunization. *MMWR* 1983;32:1-8, 13-17.

Cholera vaccine. *MMWR* 1978;27:173-174.

Diphtheria, tetanus, and pertussis: Guidelines for vaccine prophylaxis and other preventive measures. Immunization Practices Advisory Committee. *MMWR* 1985;34:405-414, 419-426.

Recommendations for protection against viral hepatitis. *MMWR* 1985; 34:313-324, 329-335.

Prevention and control of influenza. *MMWR* 1985;34:261- 268, 273-275.

Revised recommendations for preventing malaria in travelers to areas with chloroquine-resistant *Plasmodium falciparum. MMWR* 1985;3:185-190, 195.

Recommendation of the Immunization Practices Advisory Committee (ACIP). Measles prevention. *MMWR* 1982;31:217-224, 229-231.

Meningococcal vaccines. *MMWR* 1985;34:255-259.

Recommendations of the Immunization Practices Advisory Committee (ACIP). Mumps vaccine. *MMWR* 1982;31:617-620, 625.

Supplementary statement of contraindications to receipt of pertussis vaccine. *MMWR* 1984;33:169-171.

Recommendation of the Immunization Practices Advisory Committee (ACIP). Plague vaccine. *MMWR* 1982;31:301- 304.

Update: Pneumococcal polysaccharide vaccine usage – United States. *MMWR* 1984;33:273-276, 281.

Poliomyelitis prevention. *MMWR* 1982;31:22-26, 31-34.

Rabies prevention – United States, 1984. *MMWR* 1986; 33:393-402, 407-408.

Rubella prevention. *MMWR* 1984;33:301-310, 315-318.

Smallpox vaccine. *MMWR* 1985; 34:341-342.

Typhoid vaccine. *MMWR* 1978;27:231-233.

Varicella-zoster immune globulin for the prevention of chickenpox. *MMWR* 1984;33:84-90, 95-100.

Yellow fever vaccine. *MMWR* 1984;32:679-682, 687-688.

Travel Advice and Medical Care Abroad

When medical care is needed outside the United States, travel agents or US embassies or consulates can provide names of hospitals or physicians when the illness occurs or before the patient leaves the United States. Agencies and commercial services provide advice to physicians and travelers or can arrange medical evacuation. Some agencies have toll-free telephone numbers. A list of some of those agencies follows.

ARM Coverage of New York
120 Mineola Boulevard
PO Box 310
Mineola, NY 11501

Assist-Card
347 Fifth Avenue
New York, NY 10016

Health Care Abroad
923 Investment Building
1511 K Street, NW
Washington, DC 20006

Intermedic
777 Third Avenue
New York, NY 10017

International Association for Medical Assistance to Travelers (IAMAT)
736 Center Street
Lewiston, NY 14092

International SOS Assistance
Box 11568
Philadelphia, PA 19116

Nationwide/Worldwide Emergency Ambulance Return (NEAR)
1900 North MacArthur Boulevard
Oklahoma City, OK 73127

Physicians Air Transport International
PO Box 67
Northampton, MA 01061

The Travelers Insurance Company Ticket and Travel Plans
1 Tower Square
Hartford, CT 06183-5040

Provincial health departments in Canada

Provincial health departments can provide the same kinds of services provided by state health departments in the United States.

Director, Communicable Disease Control and Epidemiology
Alberta Social Services and Community Health
10105 109th Street
Edmonton, Alberta T1J 1M8

Director, Epidemiology Branch
Ministry of Health
Vancouver, British Columbia V6J 4M3

Director, Communicable Disease Control
Department of Health
831 Portage Avenue
Winnipeg, Manitoba R3G 0N6

Director, Public Health Services
Department of Health
Carleton Place
PO Box 6000
Fredericton, New Brunswick E3B 5H1

Chief Medical Officer
Medical Services Division
Department of Health
PO Box 4750
Confederation Building
St. Johns, Newfoundland A1C 5T7

Infectious Disease Control Unit
Medical Services, Health and Welfare, Canada
Northwest Territories Region
Bag Service 7777
Yellowknife, Northwest Territories X1A 2R3

Provincial Epidemiologist
Community Health Services
Department of Public Health
Box 488, Provincial Building
Halifax, Nova Scotia B3J 2R8

134

Medical Officer of Health
Department of Health and Social Services
PO Box 2000
Charlottetown, Prince Edward Island C1A 7N8

Senior Medical Consultant
Disease Control and Epidemiology Service
Ontario Ministry of Health
5th Floor, 15 Overlea Blvd
Toronto, Ontario M4H 1A9

Directeur Général de la Santé
Ministère des Affaires Sociales
1075 Chemin
Sainte Foy,
Quebec G1S 2M1

Director, Division of Communicable Disease
Saskatchewan Health
3475 Albert Street
Regina, Saskatchewan S4S 6X6

Infectious Disease Control Officer
Yukon Region
Whitehorse General Hospital
5 Hospital Road
Whitehorse, Yukon Territory Y1A 3H7

Publications

Monthly

Caribbean Epidemiology Center (CAREC) Surveillance Report
PO Box 164
Port-of-Spain, Trinidad, West Indies

Dengue Surveillance Summary
San Juan Laboratories
Centers for Disease Control
GPO Box 4532
San Juan, PR 00936

Epidemiological Bulletin
Pan American Health Organization
525 23rd Street NW
Washington DC 20037

Weekly

Morbidity and Mortality Weekly Report
Centers for Disease Control
Atlanta, GA 30333

Summary of Health Information for International Travel
US Department of Health and Human Services
Public Health Service
Centers for Disease Control
Atlanta, GA 30333

Weekly Epidemiological Record (Relevé Épidémiologique Hebdomadaire)
World Health Organization
Geneva, Switzerland
Telegrams: EPIDNATIONS GENEVA   Telex: 27821
Irregular

Advisory Memoranda (DQ-CPS)
US Public Health Service
Centers for Disease Control
Atlanta, GA 30333
Books

Beaver PC, Jung RC: *Animal Agents and Vectors of Human Disease,* ed 5. Philadelphia, Lea & Febiger, 1985.

Beaver PC, Jung RC, Cupp EW: *Clinical Parasitology,* ed 9. Philadelphia, Lea & Febiger, 1984.

Behrman RE, Vaughn VC III (ed); Nelson WE (sr ed): *Nelson Textbook of Pediatrics,* ed 12. Philadelphia, WB Saunders Co, 1983.

Benenson AS (ed): *Control of Communicable Diseases in Man,* ed 14. Washington, American Public Health Association, 1985.

Health Information for International Travel. Atlanta, Centers for Disease Control, US Public Health Service, Dept of Health and Human Services, 1985, revised annually.

Mandell GL, Douglas, RG Jr, Bennett JE (eds): *Principles and Practice of Infectious Diseases,* ed 2. New York, John Wiley & Sons, 1985.

Manson-Bahr P, Apted FIC: *Manson's Tropical Diseases,* ed 18. Philadelphia, WB Saunders Co, 1982.

Most H (ed): *Health Hints for the Tropics.* Wheaton, Maryland, American Society of Tropical Medicine and Hygiene, 1986.

Petersdorf RG, Adams RD, Braunwald E, et al (eds): *Harrison's Principles of Internal Medicine,* ed 10. New York, McGraw-Hill Book Co, 1983.

Prevention of Malaria in Travelers, 1982. Atlanta, US Department of Health and Human Services, Public Health Service, Centers for Disease Control, Center for Infectious Diseases, Parasite Disease Division, 1982.

Strickland GT: *Hunter's Tropical Medicine,* ed 6. Philadelphia, WB Saunders Co, 1984.

Vaccination Certificate Requirements for International Travel and Health Advice for Travellers. Geneva, World Health Organization, 1985, revised annually. Available from WHO Publications Centre USA, 49 Sheridan Avenue, Albany, NY 12210.

Warren KS, Mahmoud AAF (eds): *Geographic Medicine for the Practitioner. Algorithms in the Diagnosis and Management of Exotic Diseases.* Chicago, University of Chicago Press, 1985.

Warren KS, Mahmoud AAF (eds): *Tropical and Geographical Medicine.* New York, McGraw-Hill Book Co, 1984.

Wyngaarden JB, Smith LH (eds): *Cecil's Textbook of Medicine,* ed 17. Philadelphia, WB Saunders Co, 1985.

Index